must-see
SOUTH AFRICA

P9-CAP-916

CONTENTS

Published by Thomas Cook Publishing
The Thomas Cook Group Ltd
PO Box 227, Thorpe Wood
Peterborough PE3 6PU
United Kingdom

Telephone: 01733 503571
E-mail: books@thomascook.com

Text: © The Thomas Cook Group Ltd 2000
Maps: © The Thomas Cook Group Ltd 2000

ISBN 1 841570 46 X

Distributed in the United States of America by the Globe Pequot Press,
PO Box 480, Guilford, Connecticut 06437, USA.

Distributed in Canada by Whitecap Books, 351 Lynn Avenue,
North Vancouver, British Columbia, Canada V7J 2C4.

Distributed in Australia and New Zealand by Peribo Pty Limited,
58 Beaumont Road, Mt Kuring-Gai, NSW, 2080, Australia.

Publisher: Stephen York
Commissioning Editor: Deborah Parker
Map Editor: Bernard Horton

Series Editor: Christopher Catling

Written and researched by: Melissa de Villiers

Cover photograph: South Africa Tourism Board

must-see
SOUTH AFRICA

MELISSA DE VILLIERS

Getting to know South Africa

GETTING TO KNOW SOUTH AFRICA

Discovering South Africa

In April 1994, South Africa was reborn. After 40 years of white minority rule, the black majority won its freedom, led by a man who had been held in prison for 27 years.

Starved of tourists for decades (many people were put off visiting, thanks to the apartheid regime), South Africa's transformation from international pariah to favourite holiday destination is now complete. The 1990s have seen a veritable explosion in the international tourist market as visitors pour in, eager to see this extraordinary country for themselves.

Super natural

For many, top billing goes to South Africa's tremendous **natural beauty**. There's a terrific range of landscapes to explore here, from the dark, dreaming **forests** of the

Tsitsikamma to the red Kalahari **desert**, from the surreal **sandstone cliffs** of the Golden Gate Park to the **coral reefs** of jungly northern Maputaland.

If it's **beaches** you're after, there are over 1000km of them – uncrowded and sandy. Wildlife? South Africa has more than 500 **game farms and parks**, including the majestic Kruger, one of the world's best-known reserves. What's more, from the **vineyards** at the foot of Africa to high-voltage Johannesburg, the internal transport network is excellent, and the weak rand means that visitors can expect very good value for money.

Green's the word

The conservation issue has played a big part in debates as the 'New South Africa' gets underway. Both the government and big business have invested heavily in '**ecotourism**' projects, whereby farmland is restocked with indigenous flora and wildlife and transformed into luxury private game reserves.

Stays don't come cheap, but these reserves do generate much-needed jobs, channelling some of the economic benefits of tourism to underdeveloped communities while giving locals a real incentive to preserve the national heritage. For visitors keen on seeing big game, of course, it simply means that the range of what's on offer is widening all the time.

Rainbow culture

There are other, previously hidden, sides to the Rainbow Nation which are only now being allowed to shine out. Switch on the radio in South Africa today and you'll find broadcasts coming at you in all 11 official languages: English, Afrikaans, Zulu, Xhosa, Venda, Tswana, Tsonga, Northern Sotho, Southern Sotho, Swazi and Ndebele. Instead of having to play down their country's volatile history, today the South Africans are embracing and taking stock of an asset they have always had – an unusually rich **cultural heritage**.

With the whole issue of ethnicity slowly becoming less of a political hot potato, there is now official support for all aspects of black culture, from music, art, theatre and dance to traditional healing. A good way to get a glimpse of all this is by visiting one of the **'cultural villages'** which have been established around the country to promote the crafts and customs of the various indigenous peoples.

In other words, the one thing you shouldn't pack is the preconception of a nation simply divided into black and white. Nothing is that straightforward in South Africa – it's a far more fascinating place than that.

A day in the life of South Africa

*The first thing you notice on the drive in to Cape Town from the airport is the city's splendid natural backdrop – majestic Table Mountain, often bewitchingly wreathed in cloud. But it's not the only eye-opener for first-time visitors. While at first this airport road seems like any other in any other Western city, a glance out of the car window quickly dispels that view. Set back from the road behind a sagging fence is a sprawling mess of corrugated-iron and cardboard shacks, stretching into the distance as far as the eye can see. This is Khayelitsha, a black township – **apartheid's legacy**.*

The shadow of the past

Since those heady days in 1994 when Nelson Mandela led the ANC to victory in the country's first non-racial election, South Africa's division into white and black areas remains surprisingly little touched. The **poverty** of the townships, too, is practically unchanged – while there is more clean water than before, electricity and sanitation are conspicuous by their absence. **Unemployment** generally is 30 per cent, much more in squatter camps like Khayelitsha. Standards of primary education are still dismal; **violent crime** endemic. **AIDS**, too, is widespread, with one in four township adults suffering from the virus.

● *Pretoria's Union Building, seat of political power*

Reconciliation vs transformation

This is not to imply that major social and economic reform is not underway. It is – but it has not so far been the government's top priority. The overwhelming task in 1994 was to make sure that the economy did not collapse, and so a **conservative fiscal policy** was established to reassure financial markets, convince white business not to leave, and woo foreign investors. The message of reconciliation that Mandela stood for was just as vital for the nation's economic health as it was a moral imperative.

Voted back into power with a comfortable majority in the 1999 elections, the ANC clearly still has prestige. Yet it's just as clear that Mandela's successor, Thabo Mbeki, has his work cut out for him. For one thing, he must walk a tightrope between those who say the government is not doing enough to transform the townships, and those who accuse it of not addressing white fears (it is white-owned business and white individuals who currently pay the taxes and have most of the skills).

Meanwhile, black South Africans are demanding a **redistribution of resources** on a large scale, from land to civil service and private sector jobs, and the ownership of businesses large and small. Foreign investment has been slow to materialise while violent crime has increased – further discouraging investment, but encouraging whites to emigrate. The ANC's reputation has also been tarnished by charges of corruption.

Facing the future

Yet South Africa has come an extraordinarily long way since 1994. Blacks have for the first time been able to study, work and move freely in their own country. Unlike much of the rest of the African continent, there is a **democratic constitution** here, a **lively civil society**, and a robustly **independent press**. Idealism has given way to the more tedious business of rebuilding the nation – and the growing realisation that the time needed to redress the inequalities of 350 years of white domination will be measured in decades, not years.

Yesterday and tomorrow

*Although apartheid was undoubtedly one of the darkest chapters in South Africa's history, it was by no means the bloodiest. The first European colony at the Cape was established by the **Dutch** in 1652, in order to supply their India-bound fleets with fresh water and vegetables. Thanks to superior weaponry, the Dutch met with little resistance from the Cape's indigenous inhabitants, the nomadic **Khoisan**. But the fast-growing settlement at Cape Town did eventually attract the attention of the **British**, by 1800 the world's mightiest industrial and naval power. India was at the heart of the British Empire, and so in 1815 – to protect the sea route to India – Britain took the Cape from the Dutch.*

Claiming the land

A network of British-settled farms and villages soon spread through the interior as far as the Kei River, despite fierce resistance from the **Xhosa** people – black farmers whose traditional lands these were. Meanwhile, deeply unhappy with 'liberal' British rule, some 14,000 Dutch farmers ('**Boers**' in Afrikaans) left the Cape colony in 1836 and trekked away into the interior. They, too, clashed bloodily with the indigenous peoples (chiefly the **Ndebele** and the **Zulus**) whose lands they claimed on their journey north.

By 1850, the Boers had created two independent states, the **Orange Free State** and the **South African Republic** (SAR). Britain had established another colony in Natal to protect Durban harbour from falling into Boer hands. In between lay innumerable black kingdoms and chiefdoms, few roads, fewer railways. Even at this stage, South Africa was more undeveloped backwater than unified nation.

Gold, diamonds – and war

Then in 1867 **diamonds** were found just north of the Orange River (on land subsequently annexed by Britain), and the country's **industrial revolution** finally took off. However, the discovery in 1886 of huge deposits of **gold** on the Witwatersrand – right in the middle of the SAR – proved a major threat to Britain's regional supremacy. Her efforts to gain control of the gold fields precipitated the **Anglo-Boer War** 1899–1902, and a harsh defeat for the Boers.

The rise of nationalism

When the Afrikaner-backed **National Party** swept to power in 1948, it did not create **apartheid** – that was already implicit in the way the country had been governed since Union (the creation of a single South Africa) in 1910. But it was the Nationalists who took all the discriminatory legislation and refined it into a systematic body of law.

Yet the first half of the 20th century had also seen a flowering of **black nationalism,** with first the **South African Native National Congress** and later the **African National Congress** nourishing opposition to white rule. Confrontation was inevitable; the stage set for a four-decade-long tragedy with many acts.

African renaissance

Time has moved on. For all its volatile history, South Africa's transition to black majority rule in 1994 took place without the predicted bloodbath. Now embracing its **African heritage** for the first time, the country is building bridges with neighbouring nations and hopes to play a key role putting Africa's case in global forums, too. Commentators predict that if stability could only be assured, it could also become an **African economic powerhouse**, kick-starting new growth continent-wide. The pitfalls are many, but the potential is undoubtedly there.

People and places

With the richest musical history and the best-developed recording industry on the continent, South Africa's township music is one of its best exports. Locals adore it – especially jazz, which has produced some true giants. Best known among jazz buffs is the great Hugh Masekela, master of the trumpet, but there are many others, notably Cape Town's Abdullah Ibrahim. Durban pianist Bheki Mseleku and saxophonist Zim Ngqawana are just two names from a whole new generation of rising stars.

However, South Africa's music scene is characterised by the most complex profusion of styles. Take the instantly recognisable *a cappella* folk harmonies of KwaZulu-Natal's Ladysmith Black Mambazo, for example – their contribution to Paul Simon's 1987 *Graceland* album made them world-famous, but they've been wowing audiences at home since 1970. Then there's Johannesburg pop singer Brenda Fassie, who first opened the way for black women singing in the township *mpantsula* groove in the 1980s – she's still producing best-selling albums and performing to packed houses country-wide. And let's not forget Lucky Dube, dubbed 'the natural successor to Bob Marley', who blends reggae beats with *mbaqanga*-based keyboards and back-up vocals. He, too, has a huge following across the African continent and around the world.

Prize assets

Grande dame of South African literature and widely recognised as one of the world's most distinguished novelists, Johannesburg's Nadine Gordimer was awarded the Nobel Prize for Literature in 1991, the first South African woman ever to receive it. Fellow Nobel laureates include

Anglican churchman Desmond Tutu and, of course, Nelson Mandela, who shared his 1993 Peace Prize with South Africa's then premier, the Afrikaner Nationalist F W de Klerk.

Playing the game

Since South Africa's readmittance to the international sporting arena in 1994, all sorts of successes have come this sports-mad country's way. In 1996, the year of the Atlanta Olympics, marathon runner Josiah Thugwane stunned everyone by taking the gold medal, and swimmer Penny Heyns struck gold twice – in the 100m and 200m breaststroke. Golfer Ernie Els, winner of the US Open in 1994 and 1997, is consistently ranked among the world's top three players, while with more than 300 Test wickets to his name, bowler Allan Donald is the all-time South African cricketing record-holder.

Picture this

Drawing on traditional African forms as diverse as beadwork and mask-making along with contemporary Western trends, South African art is richly eclectic. Two of the most exciting figurative painters around are Johannesburg's William Kentridge and Western Caper Penny Siopis, who first came to prominence in the turbulent 1980s – Kentridge's highly original take on the world, in particular, is usually linked to a socio-political theme. Then there is the formally-untrained Jackson Hlungwane from rural Venda, whose phenomenal sculptures reflect a highly-charged religious cosmology, a blend of ancestor-worship and rastafarianism. Gauteng sculptor Ezrom Legae, meanwhile, is one of a new generation of black artists whose work embodies a synthesis of both Western and African traditions.

Getting around

*Although by African standards South Africa's internal infrastructure is excellent, the public transport network is fairly limited. It doesn't link towns and places of interest effectively, so to get the most out of your trip it's strongly recommended that you hire a car. If you don't want to drive in the main city centres, metered taxis (see **Taxis** below) are your best bet.*

Air

While internal air fares are relatively expensive, booking tickets as far in advance as possible means you can take advantage of any special deals. The largest domestic carrier is **South African Airways** (SAA) and its subsidiary, **SA Express**. If you're planning to take more than four (but fewer than eight) internal flights, SAA issues a handy **African Explorer** pass which can work out a lot cheaper than buying tickets separately. *Central reservations, tel: 0027 11 4799; UK reservations, tel: (0171) 312 5000.*

Other domestic airlines include **Comair**, who operate in conjunction with British Airways (*tel: 0027 11 921 0222*) and **Sun Air** (*tel: 0027 11 923 6400*), who fly only between Johannesburg, Cape Town and Durban.

Buses

Travel by long-distance bus (they're known as 'coaches' here) is safe and good value. The two main bus companies link most towns and cities: **Greyhound Coach Lines** (*tel: 0027 11 830 1400*) and **Translux** (*tel: 0027 11 774 3333*). Tickets must be booked at least 24 hours in advance. Other long-distance services are offered by **Intercape** (*tel: 0027 21 386 4444*) and **Springbok Atlas** (*tel: 0027 21 448 6545*).

Car hire

All the major international car-hire companies have offices at Johannesburg, Cape Town, Durban and Port Elizabeth airports and downtown as well. Hiring a car is a relatively expensive option, but booking in advance through your tour operator or travel agent could get you a better deal. Check that your travel insurance covers you for driving on gravel roads – don't assume it will. Usually a **minimum age** (23 or even 25) is specified, and you'll also need an **international drivers' licence**, which

must carry the photograph as well as the signature of the holder. Any of the major motoring organisations in your own country will be able to arrange this for you.

Driving

Thanks to its extensive, relatively uncrowded road network and low fuel prices, South Africa is a great country to explore by car. However, there is a gruesomely high **road accident rate**, and you should be extremely vigilant at all times. In rural areas, watch out for animals on the roads, especially at night.

Traffic drives on the left. The **speed limit** is 100kmh on rural roads, 120kmh on freeways and 60kmh in towns and other built-up areas – and seat belts are compulsory.

Petrol stations are plentiful on major routes, infrequent on others. Main stations open for 24 hours, otherwise 0700–1900. The usual fuel in coastal areas is 97 octane, on the Highveld, 93 octane, while unleaded petrol is now becoming more widely available.

Remember that credit cards are *rarely* accepted as **payment for fuel**, so you must carry **cash**. It's also a good idea to keep a supply of small denomination notes and coins handy for the road tolls you may come across on certain main highways.

Safety tips for drivers:

- **Route direction** signs are located on the far side of junctions, not

on the near side as in the UK, so anticipate turn-offs in plenty of time.

- Be prepared for '**four-way stop**' road junctions (signposted) where you have to stop, even if there is no other traffic. Vehicles proceed across the intersection in the order they arrived.

- On main roads, slower vehicles are expected to give way to faster traffic by pulling over onto the hard shoulder or **emergency lane**. Always check that this lane is clear of pedestrians, cyclists, animals or any other obstruction before making this manoeuvre.

Maps and information

Before you go

Satour
5/6 Alt Grove, Wimbledon, London SW19 4DZ. Tel: (0181) 944 8080. Fax: (0181) 944 6705.

When you're there

Western Cape Tourism Board
Tel: 0027 21 418 3716.
Fax: 0027 21 914 4610

Eastern Cape Tourism Board
Tel: 0027 406 35 2115.
Fax: 0027 406 36 4019.

Northern Cape Tourism Authority
Tel: 0027 531 31434.
Fax: 0027 531 812 937.

Free State Tourism Board
Tel: 0027 51 403 3845.
Fax: 0027 51 448 8361.

Mpumalanga Tourism Authority
Tel: 0027 13 759 5300.
Fax: 0027 13 759 5441.

Northern Province Tourism Board
Tel: 0027 15 288 0241.
Fax: 0027 15 288 0094.

North-West Parks and Tourism Board
Tel: 0027 140 84 3040/8.
Fax: 0027 140 84 2524.

KwaZulu-Natal Tourism Authority
Tel: 0027 31 307 3800.
Fax: 0027 31 305 6693.

Gauteng Tourism Agency
Tel: 0027 11 355 8040.
Fax: 0027 11 335 8049.

Taxis

Metered taxicabs can't be hailed on the street. Either book by telephone (companies are listed in the *Yellow Pages*), or pick one up from your hotel reception, or the ranks which are found at all key locations in major cities and towns.

Fares are relatively cheap, but make sure the meter is switched on at the beginning of the journey. A **small tip** (rounding up the fare to the nearest rand) is acceptable.

Trains

South Africa's long-distance trains are punctual and reasonably inexpensive, although journey times can be exceedingly long (the term 'express' really refers to the small number of stops, rather than the speed of the service). Coupés, accommodating two people in first-class cabins while second-class takes a maximum of three, are the best deal if you're travelling as a couple. If your route includes overnight travel, all trains have sleeping berths whose use is included in the fare but

you'll have pay for sheets and blankets separately (buy a bedding voucher when making a reservation, or on the train).

State-owned Spoornet operates most of the intercity routes, including the **Trans-Oranje Express** (once a week between Cape Town and Durban via Kimberley and Bloemfontein), the **Trans-Natal Express** (daily between Durban and Johannesburg) and the **Trans-Karoo Express** (daily between Cape Town and Johannesburg). *Reservations and enquiries, tel: 0027 11 773 2944.*

If you fancy travelling in real style and comfort, the **Blue Train** is a splendid luxury express service travelling between Pretoria to Cape Town (29 hours) and back three times a week. Formal dress is expected in the evenings. Other journeys include the Garden Route, and Pretoria to the Kruger Park. *Tel: 0027 11 773 7631, or 0027 21 405 2672.* Alternatively, try opulent **Rovos Rail**, which runs three beautifully restored vintage trains on similar routes. *Tel: 0027 12 323 6052.*

Don't miss

1 Table Mountain

Take the four-minute cable ride up the face of Cape Town's most famous landmark for magnificent views of the African continent's southernmost tip. Or try walking up – most of the mountain is a protected nature reserve. **Pages 36–37**

2 The Garden Route

Drive one of Africa's most famous highways, a sweeping belt of indigenous forest flanked by beach on one side, mountains and blue lagoons on the other. It's well geared up for holidaymakers, too, with good hotels and restaurants along the way. **Pages 44–45**

3 The Winelands

Get acquainted with the Cape's grape on a tour of South Africa's 18th-century wine farms, an easy day trip from Cape Town. Spend a day visiting four or five cellars, and be sure to send some cases home. **Pages 54–55**

4 Durban's beaches

A luscious subtropical coastline and year-round sun have made Durban the country's favourite holiday playground. There are beaches here to suit all tastes, from families to surfers and amusement arcade junkies. **Page 79**

5 The Drakensberg

South Africa's highest mountain range offers some truly exceptional scenery. There are hikes and climbs to suit all levels here, and you can sleep in caves where San hunter-gatherers once lived. **Pages 84–85**

6 Simunye Zulu Lodge

Spend the night in a thatched Zulu village hut, sampling traditional African food, drink and culture – an uncontrived introduction to Zulu tradition first-hand. **Page 96**

7 Kalahari-Gemsbok National Park

This outstanding reserve is well worth the trouble it takes to get here, offering great game-viewing in a magnificent wide-open, semi-desert setting. Pages 100–101

8 Soweto

Explore South Africa's most famous township on a daytime guided tour – or try a night-time *shebeen* (pub) crawl round the most colourful meeting spots. Pages 126–127

9 Blyde River Canyon

Take a half-day's drive around one of the world's largest and loveliest gorges, crammed with mist forest, tumbling waterfalls and extraordinary rock formations. Or go hiking and climbing in the nature reserve. Pages 131, 133

10 Kruger National Park

Experience one of South Africa's great wildernesses – a game reserve as big as Wales, with more mammal species than any other park in Africa. Thousands of animals and birds live here, including the Big Five (lion, elephant, buffalo, leopard and rhino). Pages 134–139

Cape Town and the Peninsula

Spread along a mighty peninsula, surrounded by sea, mountains and wide, white beaches, Cape Town has one of the grandest settings of any city in the world. But natural wonders aren't the only attraction. Southern Africa's oldest European-settled region boasts some of the most sophisticated shops, restaurants and nightlife in the country, along with a thriving arts community.

CAPE TOWN AND THE PENINSULA

BEST OF
Cape Town and the Peninsula

*Tourist information: **Captour**, Cape Town's main tourist office, is a few minutes' walk away from the main railway station in Adderley St: Tourism Gateway Centre, 3 Adderley St. Open Mon–Fri 0800–1700, Sat 0830–1300, Sun 0900–1300. Tel: (021) 418 5214. Or check out this useful website: www.capetown.co.za.*

① Groot Constantia

In the 18th century the Constantia Estate produced vintages famous the world over – in *Sense and Sensibility*, for example, a glass of 'the finest old Constantia that ever was tasted' soothes Elinor Dashwood's broken heart. Within easy striking distance of central Cape Town, the farm is now government-owned, and run as a model wine estate. **Page 25**

② The Victoria and Alfred Waterfront

Cape Town's revamped Victorian harbour now houses some of the city's busiest bars, restaurants and shops. Crowds flock to watch the open-air concerts and street performers, but it's also an excellent place simply to absorb the bustle of a working harbour, with Table Mountain as the spectacular backdrop. **Pages 26–27**

③ Chapman's Peak Drive

Winding from Hout Bay to Noordhoek over the rocky spine of the Peninsula, skirting sheer cliffs that at one point plunge 600m to the sea below, this dramatic drive is not for vertigo sufferers. **Page 29**

④ Cape Point

According to popular belief, this towering headland at the tip of the Cape Peninsula is where the Indian and Atlantic oceans meet. True or not, the superbly wild sea and mountain views still make it unmissable. **Page 31**

⑤ Table Mountain

A majestic, brooding wilderness in the heart of the Mother City, 'the mountain', as the locals call it, is also a protected reserve, offering walks through unspoilt scenery with magnificent views. No visit is complete without gaining a view from the top – a dizzying four-minute journey by cable car. **Pages 36–37**

⑥ Kirstenbosch National Botanical Gardens

Spreading out over Table Mountain's eastern slopes, these world-famous gardens offer a good introduction to the Cape's huge range of indigenous flora, and a peaceful retreat from city traffic. **Page 37**

23

Getting around:

Cape Town enjoys one of the country's most extensive public transport networks, but to get the most out of the Atlantic Seaboard, consider hiring a car. **Buses**: the main bus terminal is in Grand Parade Square, Strand St, behind the main railway station. For timetables, enquire at the **Golden Arrow** information kiosk, or call direct. Tickets are sold on board by the driver (*tel: (021) 934 0552*). **Waterfront Buses** operates a handy service from outside the Captour offices in Adderley St to Breakwater Blvd on the Waterfront every 15 minutes, daily (*tel: (021) 418 2369*). **Trains**: Cape Town's suburban trains look a bit shabby these days, but provide an efficient service running south from the city centre (the main station is in Adderley St) all the way to Simon's Town. There are some great views from Muizenberg onwards, where the line hugs the shore. Tickets must be bought in advance at the station (*tel: (021) 449 2991*). **Taxis**: equipped to carry up to nine passengers each, the three-wheeler **Rikki Taxis** are a convenient tourist service concentrating on the city centre, the Waterfront and the Atlantic side of the Peninsula as far as Camps Bay. Hail them on the street, or call (*tel: (021) 234 888*).

Historic Cape Town

Company's Gardens

Most accounts of life at the Cape begin with the arrival of the first colonial governor, Dutchman **Jan van Riebeeck**, in 1652. He planted the Company's Gardens at the foot of Table Mountain to supply fresh greens to the Dutch East India Company's ships on their journeys east, and you can still see a sliver of this venerable vegetable patch at the southern end of Cape Town's main thoroughfare, Adderley St. These days, though, it's a tranquil park, a profusion of shady oaks mixed in with exotic and indigenous shrubs and trees.

Houses of Parliament

Parliament St. Tel: (021) 403 2460/1/2. Free tours Mon–Fri 1100 and 1400, book in advance.

Surrounding the Gardens are some of the city's most impressive buildings, including the Victorian Houses of Parliament and **De Tuynhuis**, the State President's elegant Colonial Regency office (behind Parliament to the south; it's closed to the public but you can peer through the tall iron gates). But Cape Town's historic core is also a thriving late-night area, known for its clubs, bars and authentic Cape Malay restaurants.

South African Museum

25 Queen Victoria St. Open daily 1000–1700. Admission: £, free Wed.

At the southern end of Government Ave, the boulevard slicing through the Gardens, is the South African Museum, the oldest and best natural history museum in the country. Treasures include the mysterious ceramic **Lydenburg Heads** which date back to 500 AD, along with a prized San rock art display and the evocative **Whale Well**, alive with eerie underwater sounds.

South African National Gallery

Off Government Ave. Open Tue–Sun 1000–1700. Free.

Cross Government Ave and make for the Gardens' eastern border. Here, housed in an airy modern building, is the South African National Gallery. During the apartheid era, a solid collection of mainly Western art was established, including pieces by Gainsborough and Rodin. Now, though, the acquisitions policy has turned against 'Eurocentrism', and indigenous craftwork and artefacts – as opposed to curios – have finally been recognised as a fine art form.

Grand Parade Square and City Hall

Leave Government Ave and the Gardens by way of Adderley St. From here, it's a half-hour stroll down to the harbour, past handsome colonial façades uncomfortably squeezed between drab modern malls and stores. Hawkers and mango-sellers add raucous colour to the pavements. At the intersection of Adderley and Darling Sts, turn right for Grand Parade Square and the City Hall. It was from a balcony in this ponderous Edwardian building that **Mandela** addressed a jubilant nation on his release from prison on 11 February 1990.

Groot Constantia

Take the M3 south from City Bowl, then the signposted Groot Constantia off-ramp onto Ladies Mile Extension, and keep following the signs. Tel: (021) 794 5128. Open daily Feb–Nov 1000–1700, Dec–Jan 1000–1800. Admission: £.

An easy half-hour drive from the city centre leads to the **Constantia Wine Route**, three beautiful wineries which once formed 17th-century Dutch governor **Simon van der Stel**'s private estate. Groot Constantia, with its gabled manor house, is the undoubted gem, housing a museum, an art gallery and two restaurants; there are also cellar tours with tastings.

> **"** . . . the fairest Cape we saw in the whole circumference of the Earth . . . **"**
>
> **Sir Francis Drake, on sailing into Table Bay aboard the Golden Hind in 1580**

The Victoria and Alfred Waterfront

From the Victorian harbour to Robben Island.

It was Queen Victoria's second son, Alfred, who in 1860 ceremonially tipped the first truckload of stones into Table Bay to start the construction of Cape Town's original breakwater. For more than 70 years this remained one of the busiest parts of the port, playing a central role in city life.

In the 1940s, however, dwindling marine traffic brought neglect and decline, and it was only in the early 1990s that the developers – inspired by the success of waterfront regeneration projects in Sydney and San Francisco – moved in to give the old Victorian harbour a thorough facelift.

Today, thanks to its street performers, malls and craft markets, and its quay-to-quay pubs and restaurants, the revamped V&A Waterfront brims with colour and energy. It is easily the Mother City's most popular attraction.

Pick up a map from the **Waterfront Visitor's Centre** on Dock Rd, the central thoroughfare that cuts through the complex. Just northeast of the centre, behind Vaughan Johnson's Wine Shop, you'll find busy **Market Square** and the **Agfa Amphitheatre**, where free jazz or classical concerts are often staged at weekends.

A short stroll east of the amphitheatre brings you to the Victoria Basin's dockside. A bewildering range of boat rides and harbour cruises set off from **Quays 4 and 5** here, including excursions to Clifton Beach, and Hout Bay. Still others depart from the **Pierhead Jetty** in the basin's south corner, on the far side of Hildebrand's Restaurant. One of the nicest short trips is aboard the old **Penny Ferry** rowing boat (although the fare is now R2), across the cut to Bertie's Landing in the Alfred Basin. You can watch plump Cape fur seals lazily sunning themselves here on a specially built jetty.

" . . . we will together find a way to combine the many dimensions on Robben Island, and we will do so in a manner that recognises above all its pre-eminent character as a symbol of victory of the human spirit over political oppression. "

President Nelson Mandela, Robben Island, 1997

Robben Island

The Gothic-style clocktower at Bertie's Landing is the embarkation point for trips to South Africa's Alcatraz, **Robben Island**, 11km offshore. World-famous as the place where Nelson Mandela and other key opponents of the apartheid government were once incarcerated, it has been a museum since 1997. Riveting – albeit grim – tours of the island are organised by the Department of Arts and Culture (*daily from the Clocktower at 0900, 1000, 1100, 1200 and 1400; admission: ££*); visitor numbers are limited to 300 per day, so get there early. The half-hour ferry ride takes you close to the island's penguin colony, past shipwrecks and seals. On shore, you'll see Mandela's cell, the lime quarry where the prisoners were set to work, and the warders' bleak village, complete with church and South Africa's smallest bank.

Two Oceans Aquarium

New Basin. Website: www.aquarium.co.za. Open daily 0930–1800. Admission: £.

Back at the Pierhead, head down adjacent North Quay past the swanky Victoria and Alfred Hotel to the Two Oceans Aquarium. Dedicated to the unique ecosystem of Africa's southern coast, it's filled with fish of all dimensions, from jewel-like sea-horses to thuggish ragged-tooth sharks, but you can also watch sea birds and penguins at play upstairs.

The Atlantic seaboard

From Sea Point to Noordhoek.

Don't be surprised at the near-freezing seas you'll encounter on Cape Town's Atlantic beaches. Thanks to the glacier-fed Benguela current washing the peninsula's western shore, temperatures remain a decidedly brisk 16–17°C (60–63°F), even during the height of summer. Still, the beaches themselves are stunning, and they're backed by a couple of South Africa's most scenic coastal drives.

Sea Point

The M6 heads southwest from the City Bowl through Green Point and on to Sea Point, an uninspiring suburb densely packed with high-rise apartments and hotels. Here, alongside a 1km-long promenade, is the nearest decent beach to central Cape Town – although as the sea's usually thick with kelp, it's used more for sunbathing than swimming. Halfway along is **Graaff's Pool**, a nude male bathing spot and gay hangout.

Clifton

Just round the headland from Sea Point is fashionable Clifton, sheltered by the Lion's Head mountain outcrop. Thanks to spectacular views of the peninsula stretching away to the south, this suburb boasts some of the most expensive property in Africa – as a glance at the glamorous beachside homes will testify. Clifton divides into four distinct sandy beaches, each of which is numbered: **First Beach** is the most self-consciously trendy, awash with thong-sporting volleyball-players, while **Second** is for teens and bodyboarders. **Third Beach** attracts a marginally more sophisticated (and childless) crowd, while **Fourth** – packed with barbecuing families – is the most relaxed.

Baboon raids

The Peninsula is home to several troops of chacma baboons, some of which are adept at raiding cars. Don't feed them, and keep your car windows closed if they approach.

Camps Bay

A few kilometres further south along Victoria Rd, Camps Bay is probably Cape Town's most pleasant and laid-back beach, and one of the few places where you'll see a genuinely mixed-race crowd. It offers sun, shade, mountain views, surfing and swimming, and plenty of good spots for lunch along Victoria Rd, too. Parking can be a problem in high season – head for the side roads leading up Table Mountain's slopes.

Llandudno

South from here, the coastline becomes decidedly more rugged. A scenic, winding 15km drive leads to the exclusive suburb of Llandudno, where a pristine crescent of sand with rocky points provides shade and corners for privacy. Bear in mind that as the parking-lot is extremely small, street parking is obligatory during the peak holiday season – get here early to find a space.

Hout Bay and Chapman's Peak Drive

Beautiful Hout Bay, the next suburb on the route, is the centre of the local rock lobster (crayfish) industry and supports a bustling harbour – although the latter's proximity to the beach

means this is not a good place to swim. Stick to strolling: the mountain views are tremendous.

Hout Bay is the start of **Chapman's Peak Drive**, a winding 10km mountain pass offering dramatic views reminiscent of the Amalfi coast, or Big Sur. Skirting sheer cliffs that at one point plunge 600m to the sea below, the road gradually uncoils down into rural Noordhoek, an isolated settlement of horse ranches, artists' studios and upmarket holiday homes – and an outstanding 8km stretch of wide, white sand, adorned with a rusty shipwreck. To return to the city from here, continue south along the M6 until the next major junction, then turn left onto the M64.

The False Bay seaboard

From Muizenberg to Cape Point.

Fed by the Indian Ocean, the waters of False Bay are a crucial five or six degrees warmer than those on the Atlantic side of the peninsula. Consequently, Cape Town's eastern beaches get extremely busy in high season, and traffic jams along the coastal highway are very much the frustrating norm.

Muizenberg

Drive out from City Bowl on the M3 freeway through the southern suburbs to Westlake, where the road forks left to join the M4. Directly ahead is turn-of-the-century Muizenberg, the city's oldest seaside resort. The overdeveloped beachfront now looks distinctly down-at-heel, but the surf's still splendid. The trick is to get here early – and during the summer season, that means 0700. Otherwise, finding a place to park can become a major problem.

Fish Hoek

Elevated Boyes Drive (turn right off the M4 at Lakeside) runs behind Muizenberg and its neighbour, the little fishing village of Kalk Bay, all the way to Fish Hoek. With its great views and plenty of lookout points, this is the spot to come during whale watching season (June–Oct), when the southern right whales gather to calve and mate, often only metres from the shore. Fish Hoek itself also has an excellent family beach, with safe swimming at its southern end.

Simon's Town

Now follow the M4 south through Glencairn to the historic port settlement of Simon's Town, a Royal Navy base from 1806 until 1957, and still South Africa's principal naval HQ. It's a pretty little place, filled with well-preserved Georgian and Victorian architecture. One of its showpieces is the whitewashed Old Residency, built in 1772 for the Governor of the Dutch East India Company; it now houses the **Simon's Town Museum** (*Court Rd; open Mon–Fri 0900–1600, Sat 1000–1300; admission: £*), an unimaginatively-displayed collection of maritime relics.

A few kilometres further south, a fenced nature reserve on secluded **Boulders Beach** (*Nov–Feb admission: £, rest of year free*) is home to a small colony of jackass penguins – an endangered species – which nest in the thick bushes and dive for food off the rocks.

Cape Point

The M4 (and, indeed, the African continent) peters out at the **Cape of Good Hope Nature Reserve** (*open daily Nov– Apr 0700–1800, May–Oct 0700–1700; admission: £*). First proclaimed in 1936 to preserve the peninsula's rare species of indigenous protea and heath, it also serves as a breeding ground for ostrich, bontebok, eland and the elusive Cape mountain zebra.

It would be easy to spend a day here – there are some good, clearly-marked hiking trails, and safe, sheltered swimming in the tidal pools at Buffelsbaai – but the main reason tour buses make the trek is to see **Cape Point**. Popular belief has it that this towering, rocky headland, battered by frothing Atlantic breakers, is where the waters of the Indian and Atlantic Oceans meet. In fact, the dividing line is at Cape Agulhas, some 200km further east, but the site makes a superbly wild and dramatic viewpoint all the same. From the car park, it's a steep walk up to the wind-lashed lighthouse at the top, or you can take the funicular. Next stop, Antarctica.

The Flying Dutchman

Cape Point is haunted by the Flying Dutchman , a ghostly ship with tattered sails and a broken mast, doomed to sail the seas forever – a legend which inspired an opera by Wagner.

Eating and drinking

Long St's fine New Orleans-style buildings once housed brothels and pawnshops, but now it's the hub of a vibrant city centre district, packed with atmospheric bars and restaurants.

Cafés and bars

Café Bardeli Longkloof Studios

Darters Rd, off Kloof St. Tel: (021) 423 4444. Open daily 0830–2400. ££. Favoured by a hip crowd of models and showbiz types, so great for people-watching. A good spot for the first drink of the evening.

Lola's

228 Long St, City Centre. Tel: (021) 423 0885. Open Mon–Fri 0800–2400, Sat 0800–1500, 1800–late, Sun 0800–1500. ££. Friendly street café with 60s-style décor and a loyal gay following.

Long Street Café

259 Long St, City Centre. Tel: (021) 424 2464. Open Mon–Sun 0900–2400. ££. Set in a lovingly revamped Victorian landmark, this funky café-cum-deli is a great hangout for brunch, sociable coffees or after-movie drinks.

Melissa's The Food Shop

94 Kloof St, Tamboerskloof. Tel: (021) 424 5540. Open Mon–Fri 0730–2000, Sat–Sun 0830–2000. ££. Ferociously stylish coffee and sandwich bar dishing up delicious snacks and take-away deli meals.

Mount Nelson Hotel

76 Orange St, City Centre. Tel: (021) 231 000. Tea served daily 1430–1730. £££. The pale-pink 'Nellie' still basks in a grand colonial atmosphere, exemplified by the sumptuous afternoon tea.

Obz Café

115 Lower Main Rd, Observatory. Tel: (021) 448 5555. Open daily 0930–midnight. £. Relaxed, groovy hangout with a clientele that varies from grunge to glam. Serves scrumptious cakes as well as drinks and meals.

Restaurants

Africa Café

213 Lower Main Rd, Observatory. Tel: (021) 447 9553. Open Mon–Sat dinner. ££. Has an ethnic décor as exotic as the menu (Ethiopian lamb casserole, Malawian chicken), and live marimba bands, too.

Aubergine

39 Barnet St, Gardens. Tel: (021) 45 4909. Open lunch Mon–Fri, dinner Mon–Sat. £££. Muscular modern cooking, combining Mediterranean and Asian flavours with a South African twist – try the lamb and aubergine in strudel pastry. One of the city's top restaurants, much loved by the local élite.

Biesmiellah

Wale St, Bo-Kaap. Tel: (021) 23 0850. Closed Sun. £. Simple family restaurant in the historic Cape Malay quarter. One speciality's the *denningvleis*, spicy lamb stew flavoured with tamarind seed. In accordance with Muslim tradition, no alcohol is served.

Blues

The Promenade, Victoria Rd, Camps Bay. Tel: (021) 438 2040. Open daily lunch and dinner. £££. Top-class Californian-style cuisine in a light and airy setting, overlooking one of the world's most pristinely beautiful beaches. Always packed, so book ahead.

Café Paradiso

110 Kloof St, Gardens. Tel: (021) 423 3414. Open daily lunch and dinner. ££. Marvellous blend of many cuisines integrated into South African cooking: Italian pastas side by side with spicy *bredies* and sticky *koeksisters* for pudding. Outside tables have views of Table Mountain.

Cape Manna

34 Napier St, De Waterkant. Tel: (021) 419 2181. Open Mon–Sat dinner. £. Unassuming restaurant dishing up superb Cape Malay cuisine, the Mother City's speciality. Look forward to *bobotie* (spicy mince stew), *smoorvis* (braised fish and rice) and mild Malay curries, all cooked with flair.

What to try

Fish and seafood are well represented on most Cape menus. Look out for specialities like *perlemoen* (abalone), crayfish (rock lobster) and *snoek* – a metre-long, firm-fleshed fighting fish from the Indian Ocean.

Clubs and nightlife

Blue Note

Cine 400 Building, College Rd, Rylands. Tel: (021) 637 9133. Open daily 2000– late. ££. Respected jazz club featuring fresh talent and impromptu performances as well as established stars.

Coffee Lounge

Top Floor Theatre, 76 Church St. Tel: (021) 24 6784. Open Fri–Sat 2100– late. ££. DJs spin Afro-rhythms, trance and deep, funky house; also houses a small theatre and 60s-retro coffee bar.

Green Dolphin Jazz Restaurant

Victoria and Alfred Arcade, Waterfront. Tel: (021) 21 7471. Open daily 2000– midnight. ££. One of the city's oldest-established venues for live Cape jazz.

La Med

Glen Country Club, Victoria Rd, Clifton. Tel: (021) 468 5600. £. Great drink-beer, watch-sunset spot, just a 20-minute drive from the centre of town. Live music on Wed, Fri and Sun.

The Lounge

194 Long St, City Centre. Tel: (021) 24 7636. Open daily, 2100–0400. £. Busy dance venue, with resident DJs mixing anything from jazzy grooves to drum 'n' bass. Also pool tables, bar and a spacious balcony.

Ruby in the Dust

Lower Main Rd, Observatory. Tel: (021) 448 8555. Open daily 2000–late. ££. Catch a live act at this ever-popular music venue, showcasing up-and-coming talent as well as established bands.

The Zone

45 Buitengracht St, City Centre. Tel: (082) 576 8303. Open Fri–Sat 2100– 0600. ££. Hip dance space specialising in hard, uplifting house.

Tip

For an insider's take on the Cape Jazz scene, let Our Pride *show you around the city's best clubs (* tel: (021) 633 8495 *).*

Theatre, performance and cinema

The Baxter Theatre Centre

Main Rd, Rosebank. Tel: (021) 685 7880. A showcase for innovative contemporary material as well as classics.

Cinema Nouveau

V&A Waterfront. Tel: (021) 430 8020. Cape Town's newest venue for foreign and art-house films, backed up by an excellent sound system and a trendy café. Also has a branch at Cavendish Square, Claremont.

The Labia

68 Orange St, City Centre. Tel: (021) 24 5927. The city's oldest cult-art cinema, still going strong.

The Nico Theatre Centre

DF Malan St, Foreshore. Tel: (021) 21 5470. The most prestigious performance venue, with an opera house and two theatres.

Shopping

African Image

Table Bay Hotel Mall, Victoria Wharf, Waterfront. Tel: (021) 419 0382. Open Mon–Sat 0900–1700. A choice selection of African artefacts, from beaded wall-hangings to baskets and pottery.

Leslie Urry

Diamond & Jewellery Studio, 80 St Georges St Mall, City Centre. Tel: (021) 424 9270. Open Mon–Fri 0900–1700, Sat 0900–1300. The Urry family mine, cut and polish their own diamonds – and offer good prices.

Montebello Design Centre

31 Newlands Ave, Newlands. Tel: (021) 686 6445. Open Mon–Fri 0900–1700, Sat–Sun 1000–1500. Some of the city's most original artisans work from studios in this renovated stable block, producing ceramics, metal-work, pottery and jewellery.

The Pan African Market

76 Long St, City Centre. Tel: (021) 242 957. Open Mon–Fri 0930–1700, Sat–Sun 0930–1530. A fine old Victorian mansion crammed with quality crafts from all over Africa.

The Potters Shop

6 Rouxville Rd, Kalk Bay. Tel: (021) 788 7030. Open Mon–Thur 0930–1300, 1400–1630, Fri–Sat 0930–1300. Charming village gallery with informed owner, specialising in ceramics and pottery.

PROFILE

City Lodestone

Table Mountain is one of the world's most famous landmarks. Like a gigantic inn-sign promising hospitality, its flat-topped summit can be seen by approaching ships from as far as 200km away – although whenever the southeaster blows (more often than holidaymakers might care to think about), a fluffy 'cloth' of cloud quickly descends.

No visit to Cape Town is complete without a ride to the top of Table Mountain by **cable car**, a dizzying four-minute journey. Vertigo-sufferers should grit their teeth and think of the marvellous views in store from the 1086m summit: to the north, the Hottentots-Holland Mountains, and to the south, the entire Peninsula clear to Cape Point. Regular departures leave from the **Lower Cableway Station**. *Tel: (021) 245 148. Open daily (weather permitting)*

CAPE TOWN AND THE PENINSULA

May–Oct 0830–1730, Nov 0800–2130, Dec–mid Jan 0700–2230, mid Jan–Apr 0800–2130. Admission: £. Follow Kloof Nek Rd south from the city centre to the roundabout at the top, turn right into Tafelberg Rd and follow the signs.

The mountain is also a nature reserve, with around 500 footpaths up to the summit: pick up a leaflet with maps from the tourist office. **Devil's Peak**, to the left of the mountain as you look up from the city centre, and **Lion's Head**, guarding its western flank, offer rewarding hikes, too, especially when the watsonias are out in flower (Oct– Nov). Lion's Head is much the easier climb, with fixed chain-ladders to help you along the steeper parts. *Follow the signs for Signal Hill from the Kloofnek roundabout.*

The eastern slopes are graced by magnificent **Kirstenbosch National Botanical Gardens**, the oldest and largest such garden in South Africa and an excellent place to see Cape fynbos (a unique indigenous heathland vegetation) in its dramatic wild mountain habitat. *Open daily Apr–Aug 0800–1800, Sept–Mar 0800–1900. Admission: £. Also tea house and nursery. From the city centre, take the M3 (De Waal Drive, then Union) past the University on your right, and turn right into Rhodes Ave.*

The Western Cape

Small wonder this is South Africa's most popular province. To the east, the scenic Garden Route links lush forests, lakes and mountains, while the West Coast offers bleakly beautiful seascapes – and fine seafood. In between lie winelands and the wild Cederberg mountains, criss-crossed with hiking trails. With Cape Town as your base, there's a lot to explore . . .

BEST OF
The Western Cape

Tourist information: The **Western Cape Tourism Board** *is housed in the same complex as Cape Town's main tourist office. Tourism Gateway Centre, 3 Adderley St. Tel: (021) 418 3716. Open Mon–Fri 0800–1700, Sat 0830–1300, Sun 0900–1300.*

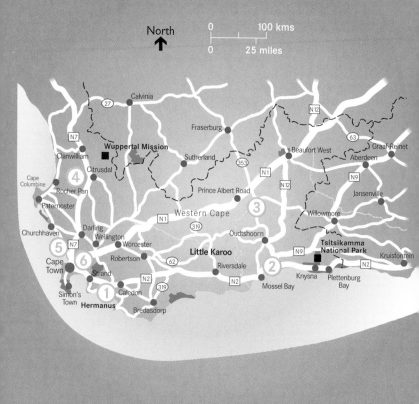

North

| 0 | | 100 kms |
| 0 | | 25 miles |

Calvinia
(27)
Fraserburg
(N 12)
(N7)
Wuppertal Mission
Sutherland
Beaufort West
(63)
Graaf-Reinet
Clanwilliam
(353)
Aberdeen
Citrusdal
Prince Albert Road
(N1)
(N9)
Cape Columbine
④
(N12)
Jansenville
Rocher Pan
Western Cape
Willowmore
Paternoster
(319)
Oudtshoorn
③
Churchhaven
(N1)
Tsitsikamma
National Park
⑤
Darling
Worcester
Little Karoo
(N9)
Kruisfontein
(N7)
Wellington
②
(N2)
Cape Town
⑥
Robertson
Riversdale
Knysna
Plettenburg
Bay
Simon's Town
①
Strand
(62)
Mossel Bay
Caledon
(N2)
(N2)
Hermanus
(319)
Bredasdorp

① The Whale Coast

Each year between June and November, the largest concentration of southern right whales on the planet come to South Africa's Atlantic coast to mate and calve. The little town of Hermanus, set on a wide, sheltered bay, is an excellent place to spot them from the shore. **Pages 42–43**

② The Garden Route

A sweeping belt of indigenous forest flanked by unspoiled beaches on one side and mountains and blue lagoons on the other, this is one of Africa's most famous highways. It's well geared up for holidaymakers, too, with good hotels and restaurants along the way. **Pages 44–45**

③ Bain's Passes

Some spectacular roads have been carved out of the mountain ranges which cut Cape Town off from the rest of the country. No fewer than ten (including the Swartberg Pass) were built over a century ago by the Scottish-born master engineer, Thomas Bain – they still make exhilarating driving. **Page 47**

④ The Cederberg

At the core of the rugged Cederberg Mountains is an unspoilt wilderness area much loved by local holidaymakers, but almost unknown to foreigners. Come here for solitude, crisp mountain air, ancient rock-art and a wealth of good hikes and trails. **Page 49**

⑤ West Coast seafood

Open-air seafood restaurants are a feature of coastal towns along this wild Atlantic shore. The menus are simple and the settings informal, but the quality's superb – look forward to fresh mussels, abalone, rock lobsters (crayfish) and linefish of every description. **Pages 50–51**

⑥ The Winelands

Most of the Cape's original wine farms (the oldest in the country after Constantia in Cape Town) lie within a 60km radius of Cape Town. With their stately 18th-century homesteads and mountain backdrops, they make a fine setting in which to get acquainted with the Cape's grape. Spend a day touring four or five cellars, and be sure to send some cases home. **Pages 54–55**

41

The Whale Coast

From Hermanus to De Hoop Nature Reserve.

The southernmost tip of Africa is a wild, shipwreck-littered coast of bleached dunes and rugged bays. Once feared by generations of sailors, today – thanks to the southern rights who gather here every year to mate and calve – it's renowned as one of the best places in the world for watching whales.

Hermanus

112km east of Cape Town.

Set on the northernmost curve of sweeping Walker Bay, Hermanus is the region's busiest resort and South Africa's self-proclaimed 'whale capital'. Not without reason: up to 80 southern rights (from an estimated world population of some 6000) gravitate here every year between June and October. The best vantage points are along the 5km clifftop path running east from the old harbour round to the lagoon at Grotto Beach. Or listen in on the whales' magical, sing-song 'conversations', transmitted live via a sonar buoy to a special room in the Old Harbour Museum (*adjacent to Market Square; tel: (0283) 21475; open Mon–Sat 0900–1700, Sun 1200–1600; admission: £*).

Gansbaai

Gansbaai, just a few kilometres further east along the R43, is an unpretentious fishing town fast winning a major reputation as a **shark-diving centre**. Boats head out to Dyer Island, some 12km offshore, where the resident colony of Cape fur seals make tasty snacks for passing great white sharks. Raw meat is used as bait, and, if there is a sighting, two people at a time can be lowered a metre into the depths inside a strong steel cage.

Great whites can weigh over 7000kg and reach a length of up to 2m; getting this close to one gives a powerful impression of a magnificent creature which demands our

respect – and protection. But make sure the tour operator you pick is a reputable one: check with the **Gansbaai Tourism Bureau** for a list of recommended companies (*cnr Berg and Main Sts; tel: (02834) 41439*).

Cape Agulhas

To reach Cape Agulhas, which officially divides the Indian and Atlantic Oceans, head inland from Hermanus on the R43 through undulating wheatfields to Bot River, then turn right onto the R316. At Bredasdorp, the road splits again; the southern fork leads 43km to Agulhas. The flat, rocky peninsula is nowhere near as dramatic as Cape Point, but at least you can say you've stood at Africa's southernmost tip. You can also climb the sturdy **Victorian lighthouse**, which has a tearoom and a small museum (*tel: (02846) 56078; open Mon 1000–1600, Tue–Sat 0930–1645, Sun 1000–1315; admission: £*).

Arniston

Some 24km southeast from Bredasdorp along the R316, pretty Arniston (also known as Waenhuiskrans) makes an easy day trip from Hermanus. The modern resort has been sensitively developed to blend in with the original settlement at **Kassiesbaai**, a cluster of thatched, whitewashed 19th-century cottages now protected as a National Monument. They make a delicious backdrop to sea bathing here – in brilliant turquoise Indian Ocean breakers, as opposed to the steel-blue Atlantic ones back west.

De Hoop Nature Reserve

Tel: (028) 542 1126. Open daily 0700–1800. Admission: £.

De Hoop Nature Reserve – another excellent place to spot southern lights – lies some 50km west of Bredasdorp along a signposted dirt track. There's good swimming off a lovely dune-heaped beach punctuated with dramatic rock formations, while inland you can see Cape mountain zebra and bontebok grazing amidst the fynbos.

Tip

*To keep up to date on whale sightings in season, ring the Whale Hotline (**0800 228222**).*

The Garden Route

A lushly forested coastal terrace stretching some 200km from the industrial town of Mossel Bay east to Storms River Mouth, the Garden Route is very much an African garden – wild, fynbos-scented and dramatic. The best sights can't be seen from the road, so take the time to head off the freeway and explore a little.

The Outeniqua Choo-Tjoe

George Station, Market St. Tel: (044) 801 8288. Departures Mon–Sat 0930, 1300. Fare: £; under-3's free; concessions for children under 16.

Gateway to the Garden Route is **George**, 66km northeast of Mossel Bay and then a 5km detour north off the N2 highway. With its leafy avenues and gracious 19th-century cathedral, it's pleasant enough, but the main reason for stopping here is to ride the **Outeniqua Choo-Tjoe**, a veteran steam train plying a picturesque 68km route past beaches, lakes and forest to Knysna. One-way trips take two and a half hours, and can be linked to a return shuttle service.

Diepwalle State Forest

Open daily 0600–1800. Admission: £. Take the N2 east to Plettenberg Bay, turn left onto the R339 and follow the signs. It's about 16km to the Forestry Station, the last 6km on gravel.

Laid-back **Knysna**, 102km east of Mossel Bay, overlooks a salt-water lagoon guarded by The Heads, an impressive pair

of sandstone cliffs. Thesen's Isle in the lagoon has an appealing waterfront complex where you can eat local oysters *al fresco*, and there's good swimming off nearby Leisure Isle.

Knysna's biggest draw, though, are its forests, the remnants of a once-mighty woodland where herds of elephant roamed. Some

20km northeast of town, **Diepwalle State Forest** has stands of giant Outeniqua yellowwoods so tall and dense it feels like near dusk down on the shaded floor. The Forestry Station here has information on hiking trails and picnic sites.

Plettenberg Bay

Upmarket Plettenberg Bay has great beaches and the liveliest nightlife on the Garden Route, with good pubs and seafood restaurants. Work off your hangover with a clifftop hike around the wild Robberg Peninsula, part of the **Robberg Nature and Marine Reserve** (*10km southwest of town; tel: (04457) 32125; open daily Feb–Nov 0700–1700, Dec–Jan 0700–2000; admission: £*).

Tsitsikamma National Park

Open daily 0530–2130. Admission: ££. Book accommodation through the National Parks Board, PO Box 7400, Roggebaai, Cape Town 8012, tel: (021) 22 2810; or PO Box 787, Pretoria 0001, tel: (012) 343 1991.

Just east of 'Plett' lies the Tsitsikamma National Park, highlight of the Garden Route. Dozens of hiking paths (including the famously tough five-day Otter Trail) criss-cross its 80km length, past river gorges choked with indigenous forest and chains of rockpools linking sandy bays. Dolphins can often be seen in the waves, and, if you're lucky, Cape clawless otters, too.

Hidden in the western section of the park at the bottom of a winding mountain pass is lovely little **Nature's Valley**, with a 5km-long beach and a few sleepy B&Bs. The **De Vasselot Rest Camp** near here has basic huts and a stunning forest campsite, within earshot of booming Indian Ocean breakers and teeming with birds.

" *[George is] . . . the prettiest village on the face of the earth.* "

Anthony Trollope, *South Africa*, 1878

The **Storms River Mouth Rest Camp** on the park's eastern edge is more accessible and developed, with sea-facing log cabins, 'oceanettes' and campsites. Forest trails lead through hanging vines and giant ferns along a rocky shore where the river has cut a steep gorge on its route to the sea: it's spanned by a vaulting 139m-high bridge.

THE WESTERN CAPE

The Klein Karoo

Separated from the Garden Route by a great band of mountains, the Klein Karoo's dry, aloe-sprinkled valleys have an understated beauty: sandstone crags silhouetted against a cobalt-blue sky; wild flowers cloaking a dusty plain; the serenity of far horizons. This is an excellent diversion if you want a short detour away from the Garden Route somewhere off the beaten track.

Oudtshoorn

63km north of George.

Ostriches have been farmed in the Klein Karoo for over 100 years. Two great feather-booms at the turn of the 19th century first put bustling Oudtshoorn on the map – its opulent sandstone mansions date from the heady days when feathers sold for, quite literally, more than their weight in gold. The **CP Nel Museum** has some interesting, if haphazard, displays on the subject. *Cnr Baron van Reede St and Voortrekker Rd. Tel: (044) 272 7306. Open Mon–Sat 0900–1700. Admission: £.*

Highgate Ostrich Farm is a popular show farm where you can watch jockeys race the big, pea-brained birds (*10km south of town on the R3228; tel: (044) 272 7115; open daily 0800–1700; admission: £*).

Cango Caves

Tel: (0443) 227410. Open daily; conducted guided tours every hour, on the hour 0900–1600, Dec and Apr school holidays 0800–1700. Admission: £.

Some 30km north of Oudtshoorn, buried in the foothills of the Swartberg range, lie the vast dripstone caverns of the Cango Caves. There's a range of tours through this extraordinary subterranean landscape, including a fairly demanding 90-minute 'Full Adventure' option that involves squeezing along narrow tunnels and picking your way up and down dozens of stairs. Crowds don't help, so if you're visiting during the peak summer months, get here early.

Bain's Passes

Prince Albert is an unusually well-preserved 19th-century *dorpie* (hamlet): a trim Dutch Reformed church guards the whitewash-and-thatch Boer cottages while icy hill-water gushes down roadside furrows. It's 70km north of Oudtshoorn over the magnificent **Swartberg Pass**, now a National Monument. Built by the great Victorian engineer, **Thomas Bain**, the road climbs 1000m over 12km with hair-raisingly sharp blind hairpins; the views from the top are – predictably – tremendous.

Egghead

Only the truly macho would order a boiled ostrich egg for breakfast in an Oudtshoorn hotel – and then polish off all 1.7kg of it.

You can return to Oudtshoorn over Bain's **Meiringspoort Pass** – equally impressive, and not quite so steep. First opened in 1857, the road crosses the River Groot some 30 times along its 17km length; towering ochre cliffs banded with milky quartz and splodged with yellow lichen rear up on either side. Midway through, a footpath leading from the car park at Ford 17 takes you down to a 60m waterfall with a deliciously cold rock pool. *From Prince Albert, take the R407 to Klaarstroom, then turn right onto the N12/R29.*

Klein Karoo Wine Route

Tel: (04439) 2556.

Where else in the world would you see ostriches side by side with vineyards? The Klein Karoo Wine Route ends in Oudtshoorn and De Rust, having wound for some 300km through **Montagu**, **Barrydale**, **Ladismith** and **Calitzdorp**. Port's the tipple to try around here – the Douro-like environment has encouraged several cellars to plant port varieties and adopt traditional Portuguese methods and styles. Try Calitzdorp's **Boplaas Estate** 1994 Vintage Reserve – it's outstanding. *Tel: (04437) 33326. Open Mon–Fri 0800–1700, Sat 0900–1300. Tasting fee: £.*

The West Coast

Developers are only just waking up to the potential of this remote, wind-lashed coast, sandwiched between the icy Atlantic and the rugged Cederberg. It's long been a favourite with Kapenaars (Western Capers), however, who come to hike and climb in the mountains, unwind in the low-key resorts, and marvel at the wild flowers which briefly transform the veld each spring.

Darling

Satirist **Pieter-Dirk Uys** and his most famous creation, 'Tannie' Evita Bezuidenhout, have taken up residence in the sleepy farming village of Darling, about an hour's drive north of Cape Town on the R27. Housed in an old railway station building painted a vibrant pink, the **Evita se Perron** theatre and restaurant venue stages daily shows; expect razor-sharp commentary on the 'new' South Africa, well leavened with humour. *Darling Station, Station Rd. Tel: (02241) 3145 or 2831. Performances daily 1200, 1500, 2100. Tickets: £.*

West Coast National Park

Park and information centre: tel: (02287) 22798 or 22144; open daily 0900–1700; admission: £.

Back on the R27, a drive of some 10km beyond the turn-off to Yzerfontein brings you to the West Coast National Park and one of the world's great wetlands, the **Langebaan Lagoon**. Over 70,000 migrant waders – pelican, flamingo, curlew, sandpiper and many others – fly in to spend the summer here; the hides nearest the park's information centre at **Geelbeck** farmhouse (*on the lagoon's southern shore*) offer excellent views. The park's demarcated **Postberg** section opens every Aug–Sept for the spring wild flower season, when you can see zebra and antelope amidst a sea of blazing colour. Ask at Geelbeck for information on walking trails and the park's two-day hike.

The bleakly functional resort of **Langebaan** on the lagoon's eastern shore offers accommodation and a good range of watersports, from windsurfing to yachting and angling.

Cape Columbine

North of Saldanha, the coastline fans out into a series of long, windswept beaches punctuated by rocky outcrops, pretty fishing villages such as **Paternoster**, and a handful of rapidly-growing holiday resorts. The cluster of nature reserves near Cape Columbine are a big draw for birdwatchers; **Rocher Pan** (*12km north of Dwarskersbos*) is most rewarding in the summer, when it's home to such migrants as flamingo and glossy ibis. This is a particularly good stretch of coast for whalewatching, too. *Tel: (02625) 727 or (022) 952 1727. Open daily Sept–Apr 0700–1800, May–Aug 0800–1700. Admission: £.*

The Cederberg

The R27 ends at **Velddrif**; now head inland on the R399 for 65km to join the N7 at **Piketberg**. From here, it's 46km over Thomas Bain's **Piekenierskloof Pass** to the orchard town of **Citrusdal** at the southern end of the **Cederberg**. The range's soft sandstone crags have eroded over the centuries into some arresting shapes (the 20m-high **Maltese Cross** is a good example), but you'll also find Stone Age rock art, amber streams for swimming in, pristine campsites and – in spring – swathes of technicolour wild flowers. The few remaining Clanwilliam cedars (these gave the range its name) provide shade.

Bokkems

Protein-rich **bokkems** *(small fish tied in bunches and dried like biltong) are a popular West Coast snack.*

Hiking permits and accommodation within the protected 71,000-hectare Cederberg Wilderness Area should be booked at least four months in advance. Contact **Cape Nature Conservation** (*Citrusdal District Office, Private Bag X1, 7340 Citrusdal; tel: (027) 482 2812*).

Eating and drinking

As far as seafood's concerned, you're spoiled for choice in the Western Cape: there's an abundance of good, simple outlets suitable for an inexpensive meal from Langebaan on the West Coast round to Plettenberg Bay. For gourmet options in elegant surroundings, head inland to the Winelands, the traditional centre of Cape cuisine.

Pubs and bars

Hermanus: Fisherman's Cottage

Lemms Corner. Tel: (28) 312 3642. Closed Sun. £. Bag a veranda seat for some good people-watching in this busy pub – the fish and chips are recommended, too.

Knysna: Tin Roof Blues

Cnr Main and St George's Rds. Tel: (44) 382 6870. Open daily 1800–0200. £. Smoky, laid-back venue where local and visiting bands perform to an appreciative audience. Live bands Wed, Fri, Sat.

Plettenberg Bay: The Lookout

Lookout Beach. Tel: (44) 533 1379. Open daily 0930–midnight. £. Lively bar-cum-restaurant, set right on the beach.

Restaurants

Franschhoek

Haute Cabrière

Franschhoek Pass. Tel: (021) 876 3688. Open daily lunch and dinner. £££. Smart, popular restaurant set bunker-like into a mountainside. Fine Cape cooking (with a Mediterranean edge) is served up in half-portions; you match dishes with wines from the Cabrière estate.

Topsi & Company

7 Reservoir St West. Tel: (021) 876 2952. Closed Tue. ££. Classy Cape cooking – tripe and venison dishes are the specialities here – overseen by the legendary Topsi Venter in her family-owned restaurant.

Knysna:
Knysna Oyster Company

Long St, Thesen's Island. Tel: (44) 382 6942. Open Mon–Thur 0800–1700, Fri 0800–1600, Sat–Sun 0900–1500. ££. Sit outdoors at the lagoon's edge and feast on fresh, juicy oysters cultivated at this enormous oyster farm.

Langebaan:
Die Strandloper

Just beyond the Cape Windsurf Centre, on the Saldanha Rd. Tel: (022) 772 2490. Open at owner's discretion, so advance booking essential. £. Open-air eaterie where a typical meal is ten courses of West Coast delicacies served right on the beach. Grilled, smoked and curried fish of every description, plus fresh mussels and crayfish.

Paarl: Bosman's at the Grand Roche Hotel

Plantasie St. Tel (021) 863 2727. Open daily lunch and dinner. £££. A clutch of awards confirm this as South Africa's top gourmet restaurant, offering *haute cuisine* in a lovely vineyard setting.

Prince Albert

Swartberg Hotel

Church St. Tel: (023) 541 1332. Open daily lunch and dinner. ££. Specialises in *boerekos* (hearty Afrikaner home cooking), from *frikkadelle* (meatballs) on griddle bread to *boerepot* (hotpot served with samp, a corn staple) and *melktert* for pudding.

Die Ou Kelder

Drie Riviere Wine Cellar, 5km outside Prince Albert. Tel: (023) 541 1908. Open by appointment only for groups of at least four. ££. Traditional Karoo fare, cooked with pride. Not for the faint-hearted though: specialities include *pofadders* (stuffed, char-grilled lamb's intestines) and *peertjies* (spiced lamb's testicles).

Velddrif: So-Verby Lapa

On the outskirts of town on the road to Dwarskersbos. Tel: (02288) 40106. Open at owner's discretion, so advance booking essential. £. Sea breezes sharpen the appetite at this open-air restaurant, with the sea roaring close by. Fresh linefish and seafood, along with traditional stews prepared in massive black iron pots.

51

What to try

Look out for *waterblommetjie bredie* on Western Cape menus – an unusual spicy stew made from a local pondweed. It's a true delicacy when cooked with lamb and flavoured with lemon-peel and nutmeg.

Theatre, performance and cinema

Stellenbosch

Spier Festival

Spier Wine Estate, Lynedoch Rd (R310). Tel: (021) 434 5423. Season runs Nov–Mar (ring for exact dates). Busy performing arts festival offering opera, jazz, chamber music, dance and stand-up comedy. Main venue's the sizeable Spier Amphitheatre.

Stellenbosch Festival of Music and the Arts

Tel: (021) 883 3891. Late Sept (ring for exact dates). The programme for this prestigious annual festival includes symphony concerts, master classes, ensemble recitals, art exhibitions and craft markets. Main venues are Endler Hall and the Conservatoire, Stellenbosch University.

Hermanus: The Whale Festival

Tel: (0283) 21785. Sept–Oct (ring for exact dates). Held at the height of the whalewatching season, this hugely popular arts festival includes street theatre and crafts, music and lots of whale-themed children's activities.

What to buy

South Africans can wax positively evangelical on the subject of rooibos ('red bush') tea. Made from a type of indigenous Cederberg fynbos, it's caffeine-free and low in tannin – but try a cup before you buy any tea as a souvenir. It remains an acquired taste for many visitors.

Shopping

Franschhoek

Kei Carpets

'Le Mouillage', La Motte Wine Farm. Open Mon–Fri 0800–1700, Sat 0900–1630, Sun 1030–1600. Stocks an interesting range of hand-knotted carpets in ethnic designs (you can watch them being made), along with general arts and crafts.

La Grange Gallery

13 Daniel Hugo St. Tel: (021) 876 2155. Open Tue–Sun 0900–1700. A mix of African and western craftwork to suit all pockets, set in a picturesque old barn.

Pat Bird Gallery

44 Huguenot Rd. Tel: (021) 876 2633. Open daily 1000–1300, 1430–1700 and by appointment. Upmarket gallery filled with original paintings, glassware and ceramics.

Knysna

Knysna Fine Art

8 Grey St (cnr Gordon St). Open Mon–Sat 0900–1800, Sun 0900–1400 in season. Enormous gallery handling a wide range of Southern African and international painters, sculptors and craftsmen.

Paarl

Clementina van der Walt Ceramic Studio & A.R.T. Gallery

Parys Farm, Van Riebeeck Drive. Tel: (021) 872 7514. Take the Wellington-Huguenot exit north off the N1; the studio's signposted 1km further along. Open Mon–Fri 0900–1700, Sat 0930–1530. Quality African crafts (cutlery, embroidery, textiles and ceramics) in a renovated wine cellar. Paintings and sculpture by top local artists are on display in the adjacent gallery, too.

Hout St Gallery

270 Main Rd, Paarl. Open Mon–Fri 0900–1730, Sat–Sun 0930–1700. Houses a broad range of work by local artists in different media, from glassware, jewellery and ceramics to paintings and sculpture.

Stellenbosch

Dorp St Gallery

176 Dorp St. Tel: (021) 887 2256. Open Mon–Fri 0900–1700, Sat 0900–1300. Gallery, shop and exhibition space featuring paintings, ceramics, sculpture and African art.

West Coast

Die Winkel Op Paternoster

Main Rd, Paternoster. Tel: (022) 752 2632. Open Mon–Fri 0900–1700, Sat 0900–1300. Celebrated farm stall, with small coffee shop attached.

West Coast Art Gallery

Church St, Velddrif. Tel: (02288) 30942. Open Mon–Sat 0900–1700. Joan Schrauwen's West Coast landscapes and collages, along with work by other local artists.

Whale Coast

Kontrei Gallery

4 Van Riebeeck St, Bredasdorp. Tel: (02841) 51129. Open Mon–Fri 0830–1730, Sat 0830–1300. Local art and craft, from paintings to mosaic tables.

The Winelands

Wine has been grown at the Cape for over 300 years. Huguenot refugees, who arrived in 1688, planted some of the world's most beautiful vineyards in the fertile valleys east of Cape Town and built gracious homesteads in the Cape Dutch style, backed by purple-headed mountains.

Today there are hundreds of wine farms scattered as far afield as the dry Northern Cape. Officially, however, the 'Winelands' tag refers only to those farms surrounding the oldest European-founded towns in the district – Franschhoek ('French Corner'), Stellenbosch, Paarl and Somerset West. Each town promotes its own tourist route around the estates; all are within a 60km radius of Cape Town. They make very rewarding driving.

If you visit only one farm on the **Stellenbosch Wine Route** (*tel: (021) 873 4604*), make it lovely **Rustenberg**, with an orchard and dairy (even the milking-shed is gabled) as well as vineyards. *Tel: (021) 887 3153. Open Mon–Fri 0830–1630, Sat 0900–1230.*

Kanonkop Estate is the undisputed leading Pinotage producer. *Open Mon–Fri 0830–1630, Sat 0900–1230. Tel: (021) 884 4656.*

Nearby **Meerlust** is an outstanding Pinot Noir and Merlot farm. Sales and tastings by appointment only. *Tel: (021) 843 3587.*

Boschendal Estate is the gem of the **Vignerons de Franschhoek Wine Route** (*tel: (021) 876 3062*) offering not only a good restaurant but the chance to indulge in a garden 'Pique Nique' before heading to the cellars to sample wines as elegant as the setting. *Tel: (021) 874 1031. Open Feb–Nov Mon–Fri 0830–1630, Sat 1000–1230, Dec–Jan Mon–Sat 0830–1630, Sun 0830–1230.*

Nearby **La Motte Estate** is a top Shiraz farm. *Tel: (021) 876 3119. Open Mon–Fri 0900–1630, Sat 0900–1200.*

On the **Paarl Wine Route** (*tel: (021) 872 3605*) you'll find the versatile **Fairview Estate**, selling delicious homemade cheeses and sausages for picnics on the lawn. Free tastings, too. *Tel: (021) 863 2450. Open Mon–Fri 0830–1700, Sat 0830–1300.*

Vergelegen Estate on Somerset West's **Helderberg Wine Route** (*tel: (021) 847 1334*) has a stunning homestead set in beautiful gardens, and a choice of restaurants. The wines aren't bad, either. *Tel: (021) 847 1334. Open Mon–Fri 0930–1600, Sat 1000–1230.*

The Eastern Cape

Once this stark, scrub-covered region was frontier territory, where British settlers and Xhosa tribesmen fought bitterly for possession of the land. Today, holidaymakers come for the fine coastline with its pristine sandy beaches, and to visit the excellent wildlife reserves which adorn the interior. Both make a good finale to a Garden Route trip.

BEST OF
The Eastern Cape

Tourist information: **Eastern Cape Tourism Board:**
Tourism House, Phalo Ave, Bisho. Tel: (0406) 35 2115.
Open Mon–Fri 0800–1630.

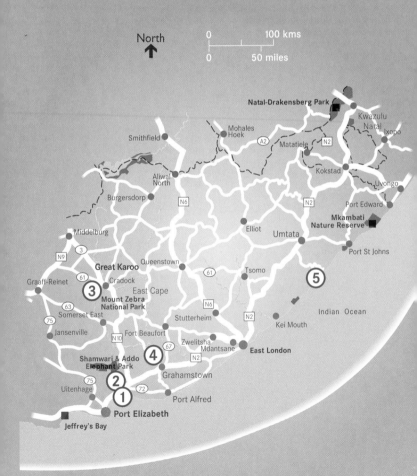

North

0   100 kms

0   50 miles

Natal-Drakensberg Park

Kwazulu
Natal

Smithfield

Mohales
Hoek

(A2)

Matatiele

N2

Ixopo

Aliwal
North

Kokstad

Uvongo

Burgersdorp

N6

Port Edward

Middelburg

Elliot

Mkambati
Nature Reserve

N9

3

Great Karoo

Queenstown

Umtata

Port St Johns

Graaff-Reinet

61

Cradock

61

Tsomo

⑤

③

East Cape

Mount Zebra
National Park

63

N6

Indian Ocean

75

Somerset East

Stutterheim

N2

Jansenville

Fort Beaufort

Kei Mouth

N 10

67

Zwelitsha

East London

**Shamwari & Addo
Elephant Park**

④

Mdantsane

N2

75

②

Grahamstown

Uitenhage

①

72

Port Alfred

Port Elizabeth

Jeffrey's Bay

THE EASTERN CAPE

① Life's a beach

The Eastern Cape's chief asset is 1000km of prime, unspoilt coastline. It offers plenty of opportunities for watersports, surfing, scuba-diving and rock and surf fishing, and while the region's low-key resorts may lack the polish of those in the Western Cape, they're usually a lot less crowded. **Pages 60–61**

② Reserve your bets

Two major wildlife reserves – upmarket Shamwari and the state-run Addo Elephant National Park – are located within easy reach of Port Elizabeth. Both are well placed to round off a Garden Route trip, although Shamwari is the only place in the Cape where you can spot the Big Five. **Page 60**

③ The Great Karoo

The San called these vast, sunburned plains 'the Land of the Great Thirst', and while it is true they get roastingly hot in summer, they also have a haunting, Badlands-type beauty all their own. Huge horizons, historic British Settler villages and a couple of fine nature reserves are the main attractions here. **Pages 62–63**

④ Peak practice

The southernmost foothills of the mighty Drakensberg range are home to some of the highest villages in South Africa. Discerning visitors come for the stunning scenery, for the rock paintings you can hike to and for the trout-rich streams, which anyone with the right rod and flies – and plenty of time – will find rewarding. **Pages 64–65**

⑤ The Wild Coast

The remote, rugged shoreline of the former Transkei 'homeland' has escaped much development, and remains the best place to find traditional Xhosa culture, little-visited reserves and superb coastal hikes through pristine subtropical forest. One of the gems of the Eastern Cape. **Pages 66–67**

A bit of rough

Drivers need to take extra care on the untarred roads of the Wild Coast, which are uniformly rough and potholed. Avoid driving in bad weather, and at night. The road down to Mkambati Nature Reserve, off the R61, is in particularly poor shape; it's recommended that you do this journey in a 4WD.

The Western Region

Traces of the British colonial past are strongly etched throughout this area, but its major draw is a superb coastline with long, uncrowded beaches, backed by several rewarding nature reserves.

Addo Elephant National Park

Tel: (042) 233 0556. Open daily 0700–1900. Admission: £. Book accommodation through the National Parks Board, PO Box 7400, Roggebaai, Cape Town 8012, tel: (021) 22 2810; or PO Box 787, Pretoria 0001, tel: (012) 343 1991.

Grittily industrial **Port Elizabeth** is the local transport hub, but there's little other reason to linger. Instead, head for the delightful Addo Elephant National Park, 72km northeast on the R335. It's home to some 300 elephants – the last remnant of the Cape's

once-prolific herds – along with black rhino, eland, kudu and buffalo. Game-spotting is from your vehicle or (if you book in) on guided night drives. There are hiking and riding trails through the dense, pachyderm-coloured bushveld, too.

Shamwari Game Reserve

Tel: (042) 203 1111. Day drives from 1200–approx 1700. Admission for day drives: ££. Park accommodation: £££.

Just 30km east on the R342 is exclusive Shamwari Game Reserve, the only place in the Cape to see the Big Five (lion, leopard, elephant, rhino and buffalo), although the lions are kept in separate enclosures. Day packages are good value, including a three-hour game drive in an open Landrover, plus lunch and a visit to an African cultural centre – but you must book ahead. There's a choice of accommodation, including the five-star-rated Shamwari Lodge.

Woody Cape Nature Reserve

*Tel: (046) 653 0601. Open daily 0800–1630. Admission: £. Follow signs
for Alexandria on the R72, then take the signposted turn-off to the right just
before you hit town.*

A short drive down to the coast brings you to beautiful
Woody Cape Nature Reserve, home to one of South Africa's
best coastal hikes – the two-day, 35km **Alexandria Trail**.
Starting out in tangled tree-and-creeper forest, the (strenuous)
route leads over a magnificent, Namib-like dunefield to an
overnight hut at Woody Cape before winding back through
forest and farmland to the base hut at **Langebos**. Advance
booking is essential, especially in high season.

Some 26km east along the R72 is **Bushman's River Mouth**
and its close neighbour, **Kenton-on-Sea**, unpretentious
little resorts packed out in summer with white families from
Gauteng. There's excellent swimming here and at slightly
bigger and more developed **Port Alfred**, another 26km east,
which also has a lively waterfront and marina.

Grahamstown

Just 50km inland lies the small, cultured university town of
Grahamstown, the best-preserved British Settler city in South
Africa; it also hosts the country's major annual arts festival.
The town's large student population ensures a reliably lively
handful of pubs and bars, and some pleasant restaurants;
this and a good range of accommodation make it a handy
place for a stopover.

No vices?

*Grahamstown's often called the
City of Saints, but not because it's
home to some 40 churches. The
label dates back to a 19th-century
requisition for tools from the local
army camp, which (allegedly) met
with the reply: 'We regret we have
no vice in Graham's Town . . .'*

Like all South African cities,
though, it's an uneasy mix of
first and third worlds. The
British-built Georgian and
Victorian buildings (carefully
restored) may look familiar, but
the black township straggling
up Makana's Kop hill to the
east is a vivid reminder of
apartheid's grim legacy.

The Great Karoo

Vast and desolate, criss-crossed by dirt roads, South Africa's sprawling semi-desert core is all that remains of an inland sea that evaporated thousands of years ago, exposing dinosaur bones and lunar-like landscapes. With its surreal flat-topped koppies *(hills) and huge skies, the Karoo is hauntingly beautiful; it's an excellent stopover* en route *to Johannesburg from the coast.*

Cradock

About 240km north of Port Elizabeth, the old military outpost of Cradock on the Fish River is now the hub of a prosperous sheep-farming district. The chief reason to visit, though, is the absorbing **Schreiner Museum** (*9 Cross St; open Mon–Fri 0800–1245, 1400–1630; admission: £*), housed in the modest cottage where the distinguished 19th-century writer, feminist and political radical Olive Schreiner lived as a young girl.

Mountain Zebra National Park

25km northwest of Cradock, off the R61. Tel: (048) 881 2427. Open Oct–Apr 0700–1900, May–Sept 0700–1800. Admission: £. Book accommodation through the National Parks Board PO Box 7400, Roggebaai, Cape Town 8012, tel: (021) 22 2810; or PO Box 787, Pretoria 0001, tel: (012) 343 1991.

It took a fight by conservationists before the near-extinct Cape Mountain zebra were granted the sanctuary of their own reserve in 1937. Spend a morning driving round the cool, high plateaux and scrub-covered ravines of the Mountain Zebra National Park for a glimpse of the 260 animals now flourishing here – along with antelope and some splendid birdlife, including both black and booted eagles.

Graaff-Reinet

Cupped in a horseshoe bend of the Sundays River some 140km to the east is the Karoo Midlands' major highlight: Graaff-Reinet. Over 200 buildings in this lovely little 19th-century town have been declared National Monuments and restored to their original whitewashed splendour; most are clustered around the historic centre. Finest of all is gabled **Reinet House** (*Murray St; open Mon–Fri 0900–1230, 1400–1700, Sat 0900–1200, Sun 1000–1200, 1500–1700; admission: £*), now an antique-filled cultural history museum.

An easy 14km drive west of town leads to the **Karoo Nature Reserve** (*open daily 0800–1630; free*) and the dramatic **Valley of Desolation**, strewn with fantastic dolerite pinnacles and domes. Black eagles glide the thermals above the rocky heights, while a lookout point offers panoramic views of the surrounding plains.

Nieu-Bethesda

Now take the N9 north out of town for 28km and follow the signposted turn-off left to tiny, tranquil Nieu-Bethesda. Here you'll find the extraordinary **Owl House** (*River St; open Mon–Fri 0900–1200, 1400–1600, Sat 0900–1200; admission: £*), a nondescript Karoo home transformed by its reclusive owner, Helen Martins, and her assistant, Koos Malgas, into a stunning example of Outsider Art. Working chiefly at night, they filled the house and grounds with hundreds of cement sculptures (sphinxes, camels, serpents and stars) and encrusted the walls and ceilings with mirrors and crushed glass. Huge-eyed guardian owls glare balefully from the veranda. It's an eerie but bewitching glimpse of a radical vision shaped by isolation.

" *The plain was a weary flat of loose red sand sparsely covered by dry karroo bushes, that cracked beneath the tread like timber . . . in every direction the ants and beetles ran about in the blazing sand.* "
Olive Schreiner, *The Story of An African Farm*, 1883

The Central Region

While the coastline east of Port Alfred is dotted with pleasantly low-key family resorts, the choicest destinations lie hidden in the mountains of the central East Cape – in the lush Amatolas to the west, and the high Cape Drakensberg to the north.

De Beers Art Gallery

Cultural Studies Centre. Open daily (in theory) 0830–1300, 1400–1615. Free.

The N2 northeast from Grahamstown leads via scruffy little **King William's Town** through the dusty scrublands of the former Ciskei (under apartheid, this was a so-called Xhosa 'homeland'). Some 65km west from 'King' along the R63 lies the **University of Fort Hare**, established by missionaries in 1916 as a black college. Although it suffered years of deliberate governmental neglect under apartheid, it has a fine track record – numerous black leaders studied here, including Nelson Mandela.

The main reason to visit, however, is the outstanding **De Beers Art Gallery**. Spanning works by pioneer painter, George Pemba as well as modern artists such as sculptor Sydney Khumalo, this is the best collection of contemporary black South African art in the country. Opening times can be erratic, so arrange your visit in advance through the University's public relations department (*open Mon–Fri 0900–1700; tel: (040) 602 2269*).

Hogsback

Now head back towards King William's Town for about 3km, then turn left onto the tarred R345 and follow the signs for Hogsback, some 27km further along up a winding mountain pass. Hidden in a dense pocket of Afro-Montane cloud forest, this entrancing little resort has fern-fringed streams and waterfalls to swim in, delightful walks through glades lined with indigenous yellowwood and Cape chestnut trees, and some great hikes in the surrounding peaks – including the Hog's Back. Booklets mapping out the various trails are sold at local hotels.

From here, it's a solid day's drive (with stops) to the Cape Drakensberg, along winding minor roads, through blink-and-you'll-miss-them sheep-farming settlements and marvellously rugged scenery. Head north from Hogsback on the R345 to **Cathcart**, and then take the N6 to **Queenstown**, a speedy 58km journey. Some 72km north along the R392 lies **Dordrecht**, where the road joins the R56. **Little Elliot** with its photogenic mountain backdrop is 106km further east, but the only place really worth a detour around here is **Denorbin Farm** (*tel: (045) 931 2232; visits by arrangement; admission: £*), home to a magnificent 32m-long 'gallery' of San rock paintings, the country's longest. You'll find it 32km outside Elliot on the R58 to **Barkly East** – a stretch which also incorporates the scenic Barkly Pass.

Steve Biko

The brilliant young Black Consciousness activist, Steve Biko, was born in King William's Town in 1946. Following his death by torture at the hands of the Port Elizabeth security police in 1977, he was brought home to be buried in the local Ginsberg cemetery.

Rhodes

Lovely Rhodes, one of the country's best-preserved Victorian villages, lies 60km east of Barkly East along the R396, a rough, steep gravel track. It has an agreeably time-warped air; few homes have electricity, while the nearest bank is back in Barkly East. In winter it fills up with piste-bashers using it as a base for nearby **Tiffendell** ski resort, an hour's drive away by 4WD vehicle. In summer, there is swimming and riding, and rock paintings you can hike to. The willow-lined streams draw plenty of fly-fishermen, too.

The Wild Coast

Named for its treacherous rocks and reefs that have claimed many ships over the centuries, the Wild Coast stretches north from Kei Mouth to Port Edward. It's a magnificently rugged shoreline, which has stayed pretty much undeveloped and remote – chiefly because during apartheid, it fell within the neglected Xhosa 'homeland' of the Transkei.

Take the N2 heading north out of **East London** towards Umtata. After 65km you cross the Kei River and immediately the landscape changes: road conditions deteriorate rapidly, while thatched, circular Xhosa homesteads dot the grassy hillsides and overgrazed plains.

Dwesa Nature Reserve

Open daily 0600–1800. Admission: £. Book accommodation through the Nature Conservation Office, cnr York & Victoria Sts, Umtata; tel: (0471) 31 2711; open Mon–Fri 0800–1630.

Continue through unremarkable **Butterworth** and **Idutywa** to the even less prepossessing village of **Jojweni** (Viedgesville), some 18km short of Umtata. A tarred turn-off leads right to Coffee Bay, with a signposted detour (on gravel) to Elliotdale. Some 20km further on, turn right at the signpost for beautiful Dwesa Nature Reserve – 5700 hectares of subtropical forest criss-crossed with trails leading to grassland and beach. Wildlife includes eland, buffalo and samango monkeys, while Kobole Point is a good place to spot whales in season. Accommodation is in log cabins on stilts, but you must bring all your own supplies – there's no shop or restaurant.

Flanked by splendid bush-covered cliffs, nearby **Coffee Bay** is a popular resort that still manages to feel pleasantly low-key and undiscovered. A lagoon offers the safest swimming, while the 1km-long beach is a big draw for surfers.

A winding 35km drive south (or an easy 8km beach hike) brings you to **Hole in the Wall**, named for its massive offshore rock shelf pierced through by a giant, wave-bored

tunnel. Smaller and quieter than Coffee Bay, this resort has safe sea bathing and some good short coastal trails, too.

Back on the N2, the road leads through **Umtata**, once the Transkei's ramshackle 'capital', now a bustling administrative centre. Take the R61 exit out of town through Libode; a scenic 90km drive through rolling grassland and traditional villages brings you to sleepy **Port St Johns**, picturesquely situated on the mouth of the Mzimvubu River. Its seductively derelict, laid-back atmosphere has made it a big hit with artists, hippies and backpackers, who come to chill out on the beaches, deck themselves in traditional Xhosa beadwork, and consume vast quantities of the potent local marijuana. **Second Beach**, 5km south of town, has the best surfing and safe bathing.

Mkambati Nature Reserve

Tel: (037) 727 3124. Open daily 0600–1800. Admission: £.

Some 40km north of Port St John's along the R61, a gruelling dirt track leads down to idyllic Mkambati Nature Reserve, the Wild Coast's finest. The scenery's wonderfully diverse: 80 square kilometres of grassland, lushly forested ravines and long stretches of deserted, rocky beach, with waterfalls and two wide estuaries for swimming and canoeing. The forests are rich in birdlife, and you've a good chance of spotting blue wildebeest, blesbok and eland, too. Accommodation is in self-catering rondavels right on the beach, or bungalows.

Transkei Traffic Lights

Watch out for the 'Transkei Traffic Lights' as you drive through the region – the little black pigs that regularly stray (without any apparent sense of impending doom) into the path of oncoming cars.

Eating and drinking

While not exactly noted for its distinctive cuisine, this mainly agricultural region does produce a handful of good, simple ingredients worth looking out for. Karoo lamb – fed on wild rosemary – is justifiably fêted for its flavour. You'll come across plenty of kudu steak on restaurant menus in the Grahamstown area, along with fresh pineapples, while the Wild Coast's the place to go for superb fish and seafood.

Pubs and bars

Grahamstown: The Monkey Puzzle

Botanical Gardens. Tel: (046) 622 5318. Open Mon–Sat 1800–midnight, Sun 1300–midnight. ££. Popular pub and restaurant in a sylvan setting.

Bathurst: The Pig & Whistle

Kowie Rd. Tel: (046) 625 0673. Open daily 1000–2400. £. Quaint little English-style hotel and pub, now a national monument.

Bathurst: The Porcupine

Summerhill Farm, Port Alfred Rd. Tel: (046) 625 0833. Open daily 1000–midnight. £. You can't miss this pineapple farm – just keep a lookout for the unfeasibly large artificial fruit squatting in a field near the entrance gates. But even if you hate pineapples, the lively country pub here is good fun.

Port Alfred: The Halyards Hotel

Royal Alfred Marina. Tel: (046) 642 2410. Open daily 1000–midnight. ££. In a pleasant setting overlooking the Kowie River, this is hugely popular with holidaying youth down from Gauteng for the summer.

Rhodes: The Rhodes Hotel

Main Rd. Tel: (04542) and ask for 21. £. This charming Victorian establishment houses an authentic South African version of a frontier saloon, complete with mounted cattle-horns and old-timers downing shots.

Restaurants

Graaff-Reinet: Andries Stockenstroom Dining Room

100 Cradock St. Tel: (0491) 24575. Open daily for dinner. ££. A tiny, seven-table guest-house-cum-restaurant dishing up the best food in the Karoo. Look forward to loin of wildebeest, kudu liver pâté, Karoo-bush-flavoured lamb – and heavenly puds.

Graaff-Reinet: Drostdy Hotel

30 Church St. Tel: (0491) 22161. Open daily lunch and dinner. ££. This hotel – a complex of some of Graaff-Reinet's most beautiful 19th-century buildings – also includes a very good restaurant.

Coffee Bay: The Ocean View Hotel

Eastern outskirts of town. Tel: (047) 575 2005. Open daily for dinner. £. Traditional seaside establishment which houses a lively pub and the only restaurant for miles around. Hearty, if unimaginative, cuisine, but at least there is usually plenty of good fresh fish on the menu. Pub lunches are also served.

Grahamstown: The Cock House

Cnr Market and George Sts. Tel: (0461) 636 1295. Open daily lunch and dinner. ££. Set in a beautiful Victorian mansion, this is the classiest joint in town, serving an eclectic range of delicious, if slightly fussy, dishes.

Hogsback: King's Lodge

Main Rd. Tel: (045) 962 1024. Open daily lunch and dinner. £. Cheerful country hotel serving simple, hearty grills and roasts and school-dinner desserts.

Port Alfred: Butler's

25 Van Der Riet St. Tel: (046) 624 1398. Open daily lunch and dinner. ££. A good bet for fresh fish, in a nice setting overlooking the Kowie River.

Port St Johns: The Lily Lodge & Restaurant

Second Beach. Tel: (0475) 441 229. Closed Mon. ££. The best food in town, especially if you're a fresh fish and seafood fan. Make sure you get a table on the deck outside if you want to toast the sunset.

Theatre, performance and cinema

Grahamstown: The Standard Bank National Arts Festival

Tel: (046) 622 7115. Website: www.sbfest.co.za. First fortnight in July (ring for exact dates). South Africa's biggest and best annual cultural jamboree, an event which sees every venue in this old Settler city – from the giant 1820 Settler's Monument on the outskirts of town to the scout hall – buzzing with activity. While the main programme features student theatre, a book fair and jazz and film festivals alongside formal performances of drama, music and dance, the Fringe attracts experimental talent. And don't miss the buskers and craft markets, either.

Kaya Lendaba

Shamwari Game Reserve, on the R342 between Port Elizabeth and Grahamstown. Tel: (042) 203 1111. Open daily as part of a visit to the game reserve. At this Xhosa village you can watch performances of traditional song, dance and story-telling. Craftsmen and women making clay pipes, wood-carvings, traditional baskets and beadwork are also part of the picture.

What to buy

Look out for the intricate windmill sculptures made from coathanger wire, sold just outside Cradock on the main highways. They're one of the Eastern Cape's most distinctive cottage industries.

Shopping

Bathurst: Isis Handmade

Kings Rd. Tel: (046) 625 0834. Award-winning handprinted textiles and folk art. Call for directions and an appointment.

Grahamstown: Dakawa Art and Craft Project

6–11 Froude St. Tel: (046) 622 9303. Open Mon–Fri 0800–1630. Stocks work by local crafters and is particularly good for prints and printed fabric.

Port St Johns: Pondo People

Ferry Point Rd. Tel: (0475) 441 274. Open Mon–Fri 0800–1630. Traditional Xhosa beaded clothing, baskets and cloth.

THE EASTERN CAPE

Star-gazing in the southern hemisphere

Astronauts may yet confirm that from space the Great Karoo is one of the blackest spots in South Africa. Along with a few isolated towns, the only pinpricks in the darkness of these vast, dusty plains are made by farmhouses. In population terms, this is the country's Empty Quarter; in astronomy terms, this is heaven. Certainly, it makes a great place for northern visitors to get their southern hemisphere bearings.

THE EASTERN CAPE

Stand outside on a clear night and find Crucis, or the **Southern Cross**: five bright stars, of which four form the ends of an imaginary cross. Extending the longest axis of the Southern Cross down to the horizon gives you the approximate position of due south. For a slightly more accurate reading, locate the **Pointers**, the two brightest stars in the constellation of the **Plough**. In your imagination, draw a line linking them, and another bisecting that line at right angles. Continue the line down until it intersects with your original projection of the Southern Cross, and drop a vertical line from here down to the horizon. This is **due south** – just don't forget to note where it falls in relation to some landmark you can recognise in daylight.

You can also use the Southern Cross to find the Milky Way's two closest galactic neighbours, the **Large** and **Small Magellanic Clouds**. Draw the same imaginary line down the Cross's main axis, and extend it about seven times. One either side of the line, you'll notice two hazy, almost misty patches. These – at roughly 200,000 light years away – are the nearest satellite galaxies to our own, linked to it not only gravitationally, but via a tenuous 'bridge' of hydrogen gas.

Alpha Centauri, the brighter of the two Pointer stars, is actually the fourth brightest star in our galaxy, while the stars of the Southern Cross lie conveniently clockwise in order of apparent brightness – Alpha, Beta, Gamma, Delta and, finally, Epsilon. And while it's only in the southern hemisphere that you're able to spot the Cross, at least the pattern stays fixed wherever you are here – even though each individual star is constantly on the move.

KwaZulu-Natal

From the misty peaks of the mighty Drakensberg to the grassy plains where Zulu kings once hunted, from subtropical resorts to sugar plantations, KwaZulu-Natal is astonishingly diverse. Yet the overall flavour is strongly African – this is the land of the Zulu, South Africa's largest ethnic grouping, while Tsonga culture still flourishes in jungly Maputaland up north.

KWAZULU-NATAL

BEST OF
KwaZulu-Natal

Tourist information: **Tourism Durban**: *Tourist Junction, Old Station Building, 160 Pine St. Open Mon–Fri 0800–1700, Sat–Sun 0900–1400. Tel: (031) 304 4934.*

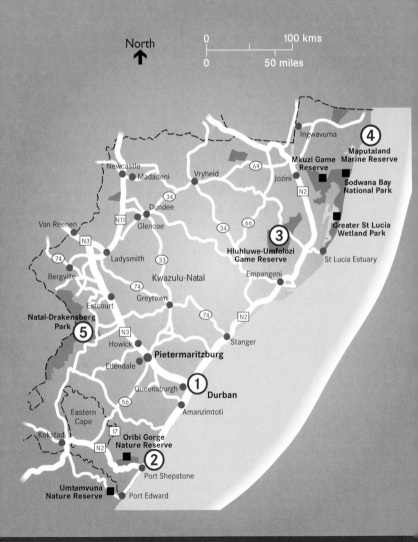

North

0   100 kms

0   50 miles

Ingwavuma

Maputaland Marine Reserve ④

Mkuzi Game Reserve

Newcastle
Madadeni   Vryheid   69
                                         Jozini
                                              N2   Sodwana Bay National Park

Dundee   34
Van Reenen   N11   Glencoe   34   66

Greater St Lucia Wetland Park

Ladysmith   33   Hluhluwe-Umfolozi Game Reserve ③

Bergville   74   Kwazulu-Natal   St Lucia Estuary

Estcourt   74   Greytown   Empangeni

Natal-Drakensberg Park ⑤   74   74   N2

Howick   N3   Stanger

Edendale   Pietermaritzburg

Queensburgh ①   Durban

Eastern Cape   56   Amanzimtoti

Kokstad   17   Oribi Gorge Nature Reserve

N2   ②

Umtamvuna Nature Reserve   Port Shepstone

Port Edward

KWAZULU-NATAL

① Durban

South Africa's busiest port is as brassy and bright as a Hawaiian-print shirt. Despite its densely packed high-rises and gritty urban sprawl, a luscious subtropical coastline and year-round sun have made this the country's favourite holiday playground – and drawn a vibrant mix of cultures, too, from Zulu to Africa's largest Indian community. **Pages 78–79**

② The Banana Express

Catch a glimpse of rural Zulu life from the windows of this old steam train, which chugs inland from Port Shepstone through rolling green hills dotted with traditional huts and smallholdings, past lush sugar-cane plantations and banana groves stretching as far as the eye can see. **Page 80**

③ The Hluhluwe-Umfolozi Game Reserve

Established in 1895, this venerable park is one of the few places in South Africa where you can enjoy big-game-viewing in close proximity to the sea. Credited with one of Africa's greatest conservation successes – saving the white rhino from extinction – Hluhluwe-Umfolozi now supports over 2000 rhino (both white and black) along with lion, elephant, leopard, buffalo and innumerable other species. Undoubtedly KwaZulu-Natal's finest reserve. **Page 82**

④ Maputaland

Large chunks of this wild region's jungly beaches, coral reefs and wetlands are protected in reserves: beachcombers, birdwatchers, divers and anglers, in particular, will be richly rewarded. **Page 83**

⑤ The Drakensberg

Snow-capped in winter, South Africa's highest mountain range offers dramatic scenery along with a range of rewarding climbs and hikes. Many caves and outcrops in these high peaks are also bright with rock paintings, relics of the nomadic San peoples who once lived here. **Pages 84–85**

Getting around

Durban: only the beachfront, town centre and the Berea are well serviced by public transport. The most convenient way to explore further afield is in a hired car.

Mynah Buses run regularly from North and South Beaches into the city centre, and to adjoining suburbs within a 10km radius. You'll find the main depot on the corner of Commercial and Pine Sts, next to the **Workshop** shopping mall (*tel (031) 309 4126*).

Tuk-Tuks: these motorised, covered tricycles carry up to six passengers, and are good for short hops between the beachfront and the city centre (*£*). Pick one up from the rank outside the Beach Hotel on Marine Parade. Or book a **mozziecab**, a handy service using customised jeeps which covers much the same range (*tel: (031) 368 1114; £*).

Cruises: the *Sarie Marais* runs harbour cruises (*daily 1100; ££*) and deep-sea cruises (*daily 1130, 1430; ££*) from the **Gardiner St Jetty**, weather permitting. You can also charter boats for parties, sundowners and lunches (*tel: (031) 305 4022*).

Durban

Well connected to the rest of the country by air, most visitors use this busy industrial port as a jumping-off point for visits to the Drakensberg and the nature reserves up north. However, there's enough to keep you occupied here for several days – more, if you get hooked on the city's glorious beaches.

Many of the nicest old buildings and museums are clustered around the compact city centre. Stately **City Hall**, built in 1910 as a replica of Belfast's own, takes pride of place on palm-lined **Francis Farewell Square** – time your visit for lunchtime and you may catch a free concert on the steps outside: a traditional isicathamiya choir, or even a reggae band.

Durban Art Gallery

City Hall, Smith St. Open Mon–Sat 0830–1700, Sun 1100–1700. Free.

The Durban Art Gallery on the second floor has a small but handsome collection which includes contemporary South African art, a handful of minor works by European masters such as Rodin, and an exceptional selection of Zulu handicrafts.

From here, a short hop by taxi westwards down Commercial Rd (or a 20-minute stroll) brings you to Grey St and the **Indian District**, with its mosques and minaret-spattered architecture. Frenetic **Victoria Street Market** (*cnr Grey and Victoria Sts; open Mon–Fri 0600–1800; free*) reeks of every kind of spice (try the volcanic Mother-in-Law Masala), while outside bazaar-traders and street-vendors hawk a huge range of goods from herbal medicines to rainbow-coloured saris.

Botanic Gardens

Cnr Edith Benson and St Thomas Rds.
Open daily 0730–1715. Free.

The lush **Berea** ridgetop, overlooking
the city centre to the west, is where
you'll find Durban's subtropical Botanic
Gardens. Along with the rare cycad
collection (*Encephalartos woodii*, no longer found in the wild)
and celebrated orchid house, the luxuriant lawns of this
Victorian haven make a tranquil retreat on a steamy afternoon.

Campbell Collections

220 Marriott Rd. Tel: (031) 207 3711. Open Tue and Thur 0800–1300 by
appointment only. Free.

A short drive north from here along Musgrave Rd, and
then west into Marriot Rd leads to the excellent Campbell
Collections museum. An imposing Cape-Dutch-style mansion
(once a sugar baron's home) houses the world's best private
collection of Africana, including such treasures as Shaka's
ivory bracelet, fine art and antiques.

The beaches

Arching in a long, blond line north from the harbour entrance,
Durban's shark-net-protected **beachfront** is the most
densely developed in the country. Heart of the resort area is
pedestrianised **Marine Parade**, a tangled strip of garish
fast-food joints, pools and amusement arcades, flanked by
soulless high-rises. A recent spate of muggings means
there's now even less incentive to hang out here, although
surfers swear by the break at **Bay of Plenty Beach**.

Instead, head north along **Snell Parade** to lovely, uncrowded
Battery Beach, or south round **The Bluff** headland, which
offers good swimming at **Anstey's**
and **Brighton Beaches**. At its
southern end, rocky **Treasure
Beach** has a pristine stretch of
tidal pools, shimmering with coral
and marine life.

“ *Durban is a neat and clean town.*
One notices this without having
his attention called to it. ”

Mark Twain, *More Tramps*
Abroad, **1897**

The South Coast

The lovely coastline on either side of Durban has been blandly, relentlessly developed for tourism – but don't discount it out of hand. If you're driving down to the rugged Wild Coast, or want a weekend break close to Durban, the South Coast in particular has several choice attractions worth stopping for.

Aliwal Shoal

Boats carrying divers from all over the world crash through the shore break at **Umkomaas**, 40km south of Durban on the N2, heading for the **Aliwal Shoal** some 5km out to sea. It's not hard to see why this 3km reef is one of the country's top dive sites – just north lies the **Nebo**, wrecked in 1884 and now lying upside down in 25m of water, along with the **Produce**, which sank to a watery grave in 1974. Meanwhile, the caves along the Shoal's seaward side to the south attract a thrilling range of marine life, including ragged-tooth shark, manta ray and moray eel.

The Banana Express

Princess Elizabeth Drive, Port Shepstone. Tel: (039) 682 4821. Departures 1000 (Izotsha), 1100 (Paddock). Tickets: £.

Pulling restored coaches built in 1903, the Banana Express steams along a scenic narrow-gauge railway from industrial **Port Shepstone** (128km south of Durban) four times a week. The winding 90-minute journey inland to tiny **Izotsha** takes in banana and sugar-cane plantations as well as beaches, while on the six-and-a-half-hour trip to **Paddock**, you roll past a restful frieze of Zulu villages clinging to emerald hills.

> " *There is a lovely road that runs from Ixopo into the hills. These hills are green-covered and rolling, and they are lovely beyond any singing of it.* "
>
> **Alan Paton,** *Cry The Beloved Country*, **London 1948**

Oribi Gorge Nature Reserve

Tel: (0331) 845 1000. Open daily 0800–1630. Admission: £.

A 21km-drive west of Port Shepstone brings you to the **Oribi Gorge**, a vertiginous rocky cleft gouged out by the Mzimkulwana River – it's 25km long and, in places, 400m deep. A steep pass descends to the Oribi Gorge Nature Reserve, tunnelling through a tangled forest canopy. There are good picnic spots along the riverbanks here, and some well-marked hikes from the car park (wildlife includes blue and grey duiker, monkeys and bushbuck). The road heading north out of the reserve leads to a series of lookout points along the canyon lip, with panoramic views.

Umtamvuna Nature Reserve

Tel: (039) 684 5013. Open daily Apr–Aug 0700–1700, Sept–Mar 0600–1800. Admission: £.

Prim little **Port Edward**, 44km south of Port Shepstone on the N2, makes a good base for the excellent Umtamvuna Nature Reserve, 8km north of town on the Izingolweni turn-off. Covering a 19km section of the Umtamvuna River (once the border with the former Transkei 'homeland'), it offers some fabulously scenic day walks down into a sandstone gorge choked with dense tropical forest, criss-crossed by streams and alive with birds. In the grassland parts of the park you'll see bushbuck and baboons and, in the spring, spectacular wild flowers.

Valley of a Thousand Hills

The classic Sunday afternoon excursion from Durban is through the poetically named Valley of a Thousand Hills, a picturesque route past folds of dramatically crumpled hills. Head inland for some 45km on the N3, following signs for Pinetown and Pietermaritzburg, turn right at the Hillcrest turn-off onto the Old Main Rd, and take the R103 for Drummond.

Northern KwaZulu-Natal

Hluhluwe-Umfolozi Game Reserve

Open daily Oct–Mar 0500–1900, Apr–Sept 0600–1800. Admission: £. Book accommodation and trails through the Natal Parks Board, PO Box 1750, Pietermaritzburg 3200, tel: (0331) 8451 000.

Leaving **Empangeni** (173km north of Durban) and its unappetising industrial sprawl behind, a 100km drive on the N2 brings you to the twin game reserves of Hluhluwe-Umfolozi, once separate, now joined by a link road. This exceptional park is credited with the saving the white rhino from extinction; it's now home to the largest concentration of rhino in the world, and just about every other species of big game, too.

The most exciting way to explore is on the three-day guided wilderness trail through Umfolozi's pristine grasslands (once royal Zulu hunting grounds), where you stand a reasonable chance of encountering several of the Big Five on foot.

Greater St Lucia Wetland Park

Open Oct–Mar 0500–1900, Apr–Sept 0600–1800. Admission: £. Book accommodation through the Natal Parks Board, PO Box 1750, Pietermaritzburg 3200, tel: (0331) 8451 000.

Monkey business

Hluhluwe Game Reserve is named after the thorny umHluhluwe monkey ropes you'll see dangling over rivers in the north of the park. Their branches were once used by local herdboys to muzzle calves during weaning.

Back on the N2, it's just 25km east via **Matubatuba** along the R618 to the busy, boisterous resort of **St Lucia**, surrounded by the outstanding Greater St Lucia Wetland Park. Some 2750 square kilometres of mountainous forested dunes, wetlands and coral reefs with **Lake St Lucia** as its glittering core, this world-class wilderness area is actually several interlocking parks and reserves. Wildlife is abundant, especially hippo, crocodile and reedbuck, but the 420 species of birdlife are the biggest draw: you'll spot flocks of white and pink-backed pelicans and flamingoes, along with kingfishers, fish eagles and storks.

Most popular of the park's hutted camps and campsites is little **Cape Vidal**, some 32km north of St Lucia resort along a rutted dirt road. Set in rolling dunes just minutes from the sea, there's great snorkelling and angling, while the excellent three-hour, self-guided **Mvubu Trail** leads through thick dune forest – alive with birds and samango monkeys – to the wetlands of Lake Bhangazi.

Three quieter and more isolated camps (**Charters Creek**, **Fanies Island** and **False Bay**) dot the lake's western shore.

Northern Maputaland

Stretching some 170km from Lake St Lucia up to the Moçambican border, northern Maputaland is one of South Africa's least-developed regions, much of it accessible only along rough dirt tracks. There's a plethora of reserves around here, all vying for the title of South Africa's best wilderness experience; one strong contender is **Sodwana Bay National Park**, 350km from Durban and well signposted from the N2. Its protected coral reefs – the world's most southerly – are home to some 1200 species of tropical fish, drawing divers all year round (there are plenty of dive shops); there's also fine snorkelling at **Jesser Point**. Visit in December–January, and you can join nightly turtle-viewing trips to see loggerhead and leatherback turtles laying their eggs on the beach. *Open Oct–Mar 0500–1900, Apr–Sept 0600–1800. Admission: £. Book accommodation through the Natal Parks Board, PO Box 1750, Pietermaritzburg 3200, tel: (0331) 8451 000.*

The Drakensberg

Slicing 1000km from the Highveld all the way to the Cape, the mountain peaks of this mighty basalt escarpment are at their most spectacular along the Lesotho border, where they best fit their Zulu name uKhalamba, Barrier of Spears. Visit in spring or autumn to get the most from the Berg – summer sees the wettest weather, enhanced by high-voltage thunderstorms, while winters are dry and mild but icy at night.

The Southern Berg

The Southern Berg is the most readily accessible stretch of mountains from the coast. Heading west from Durban and Pietermaritzburg, it's 125km along the R617 to the gateway village of Underberg, although the scenery's not quite as dramatic as it is further north. Undisputed highlight is the **Sani Pass**, a dizzying climb up to the top of the escarpment (2874m) and into Lesotho with enough hairpins for the most teetering beehive hairdo – although you'll need a 4WD vehicle, and your passport to cross the border (*open daily 0800–1600*). If you don't have the right transport, various Underberg-based companies offer tours such as Sani Pass Couriers (*tel: (033) 701 1017*).

The Central Berg

Clearly signposted off the N3 and R615, lovely **Giant's Castle Game Reserve** offers great views of three of South Africa's highest peaks, including the looming 3314m buttress of **Giant's Castle** itself. There's a comprehensive network of hikes and horse-riding trails through open meadows and valleys criss-crossed with streams to swim in, and thrilling rock art viewing at Main Caves (near the main Giant's Castle Hutted Camp) and Battle Cave (Injasuti Camp).

Open daily Oct–Mar 0500–1900, Apr–Sept 0600–1800. Admission: £. Book accommodation through the Natal Parks Board, PO Box 1750, Pietermaritzburg 3200, tel: (0331) 8451 000.

Well signposted from **Bergville** on the R74, the **Cathedral Peak** area has an excellent network of hiking paths suitable for day walks or longer trails, most leading from the **Cathedral Peak Hotel** (*tel: (035) 488 1888*). For dedicated campers, **Twin's Cave** – really a large overhang – on Cathedral Peak itself is the biggest and most popular of the Drakensberg's habitable caves. It's a particularly splendid place to wake up, with mist cloaking the valleys below and sunrise touching the surrounding peaks. *Book trails, caves and the Natal Parks Board campsite here through the Mike's Pass Information Office, tel: (036) 488 1880, open daily 0700–1900.*

Vulture restaurant

Giant's Castle Game Reserve is home to a curious vulture restaurant – a specially-constructed hide where, during the winter months, you can watch the rare lammergeier (bearded vulture) feed on meat scraps left out by park rangers.

The Northern Berg

Dominated by the magnificent **Amphitheatre**, an 8km-long rock crescent glittering with waterfalls that tumble down to fern-filled kloofs, this is the Drakensberg at its most breathtaking. Much of this northern section is protected by the **Royal Natal National Park** (*open daily 24 hours; admission: £*), reached via a well-signposted road 46km west of **Bergville** on the R74. Walking trails range from easy half-day rambles to the strenuous ten-hour climb up **Mont-aux-Sources** (3282m), with two heart-stopping ascents by chain-ladder up the sheer eastern face.

There's a good range of accommodation, too, from old-fashioned country hotels to campsites. Most sought-after, though, is the Natal Parks Board's comfortable **Tendele Hutted Camp** with its fabulous views. *Natal Parks Board: PO Box 1750, Pietermaritzburg 3200. Tel: (0331) 8451 000.*

Eating and drinking

Durban's balmy night air inspires some of South Africa's best nightlife. Morningside's Florida Rd and Musgrave Rd in the Berea are two particularly vibey areas, each with a good clutch of restaurants and clubs.

Cafés and bars

Beanbag Bohemia

18 Windermere Rd, Morningside. Tel: (031) 309 6019. Open daily 1100– midnight. ££. As a cocktail bar and place to meet fellow 20–30s, this Art Deco outfit with a casual ambience rocks on weekends. Great Eastern and Mediterranean-style snacks, too.

Durban Botanic Gardens

Cnr Edith Benson and St Thomas Rds. Tel: (031) 21 1303. Open daily 0730– 1715. £. Abundant tropical foliage, huge trees, and the most sumptuous tea and crumpets.

The News Café

Cnr Essenwood and Silverton Rds, the Berea. Tel: (031) 21 5241. Open daily 1100–2300. ££. Another modish cocktail bar, with trance and jungle music backing up the buzz of conversation.

Roxy's Café

Cnr Marriott and Cowey Rds, the Berea. Tel: (031) 309 1837. Open Fri–Sat 1800–0400, Sun 1800–0200. £. Laid-back joint offering live blues on Sunday afternoons. Transvestite 'waitrons', too.

Restaurants

Aangan

86 Queen St, City Centre. Tel: (031) 307 1366. Open lunch and dinner daily. £. Staples of the South Indian vegetarian menu include the *masala dosa* (lentil flour pancake stuffed with spiced potato and green coconut chutney) and *bhel poori* (tortilla-chip-like bits mixed with tamarind and coconut chutneys, and spiced yoghurt). Delicious, enlivening food.

Amaravathi Palki

225 Musgrave Rd, the Berea. Tel: (031) 21 0019. Open lunch Tue–Sun, daily for dinner. ££. Specialises in North Indian cuisine. Best dish is the chicken *shajahami* – a mild, almond-flavoured curry – closely followed by the carrot halva pudding.

Charlie Croft's Wharfside Diner

Chelsea Harbour, Wilsons Wharf. Tel: (031) 307 2935. Open daily lunch and dinner. £. Sit outside under umbrellas or stay indoors if you prefer it pubby. Either way, tuck into fab seafood, from calamari and prawns to curries. There's a fish barbecue on Sun.

Harvey's

77 Goble Rd, Morningside. Tel: (031) 23 9064. Open lunch Tue–Fri; dinner Mon–Sat. ££. Filled with fresh flowers and bold artworks, this hip hangout dishes up fine Mediterranean cuisine with a South African twist. Seafood's a speciality.

La Dolce Vita

Durban Club, Club Place. Tel: (031) 301 8161. Open lunch Mon–Fri, dinner Mon–Sat. £££. Set in a beautiful listed building with veranda tables over the bay. The menu's Italian classics, with the accent on fresh produce. Good wine list, too.

Ulundi

Royal Hotel, 267 Smith St. Tel: (031) 304 0331. Open lunch Mon–Fri, dinner Mon–Sat. £££. This luxury hotel – a Durban institution – prides itself on offering the 'Last Outpost of the British Empire' experience; whatever your views are on that, this restaurant (one of three here) serves some of the finest curries in town.

Zanzi's

The Bat Centre, 5 Maritime Place, Small Craft Harbour, Esplanade. Tel: (031) 368 2029. Closed Mon. ££. Offers 'rainbow cuisine', so look forward to a wide range of hearty, meaty dishes served on *samp* (cornmeal) or *phuthu*, with sweet potatoes, pumpkin and green beans on the side.

What to try

The *bunny chow* – half a loaf of white bread hollowed out and filled with curry – is unique to Durban. Dennis's Spice Bar in Victoria Market is widely regarded as the finest purveyor of this legendary snack, but get there early – he's usually sold out by 1430.

Clubs and nightlife

Axis

Cnr Gillespie St and Rutherford Rd. Tel: (031) 332 2603. Open Wed, Fri, Sat 2100–0300. ££. Popular gay club offering hardcore house and 80s' classics; also hosts drag pageants on occasions.

Crash!

Main Concourse, Durban Station. Tel: (031) 361 7791. Open Wed, Fri 2100–0600. ££. Two dance floors for an all-night feast of garage, house and new disco.

Jubes

Jubilee Hall, University of Natal, Princess Alice Ave. Tel: (031) 260 1047. Open Fri–Sat 0830–midnight, Sun 1500–1800. ££. One of the best places in town to hear live jazz.

Red Eye

Durban Art Gallery, City Hall, Smith St. Tel: (031) 300 6238. Open first Fri of the month. ££. Draws an eclectic mix of artists, fashion victims, hippies and rastas for performance art and great music, from kwaito to drum 'n' bass.

Stringfellas

Durban beachfront. Tel: (031) 332 8951. ££. Call for details. This otherwise deeply uncool disco regularly hosts terrific Sunday-night *bhangra* bashes where the local Indian community gather – the women in all their exotic finery – for a celebration of traditional Punjabi music, modishly mixed with reggae, techno and disco sounds.

Theatre, performance and cinema

Bartle Arts Trust (BAT) Centre

45 Maritime Place, Small Craft Harbour, Esplanade. Tel: (031) 332 0451. Open Tue–Fri 0830–1630, Sat–Sun 0900–1700. Innovative community arts complex with dance and drama studios plus craft galleries and shops. The BAT Deck venue here hosts free sundowner jazz concerts every Friday.

Durban Playhouse Theatre Complex

Cnr St Thomas and Smith Sts, City Centre. Tel: (031) 369 9555. Call for programme details. An opera house and five theatres, including The Cellar, Durban's oldest and busiest 'supper theatre' venue.

Elizabeth Sneddon Theatre

University of Natal, King George V Ave. Tel: (031) 260 2506. Call for programme details. Hosts a wide range of cultural events, including South Africa's largest alternative film festival every June.

Shopping

African Art Centre

Tourist Junction, Old Station Building, 160 Pine St, City Centre. Tel: (031) 304 7915. Open Mon–Fri 0830–1700, Sat 0900–1300. Gallery and shop promoting quality KwaZulu-Natal art and crafts, as opposed to curios. Sculpture, painting, ceramics and embroidered and beaded cloths.

Durban Designer Emporium

77 Musgrave Rd, the Berea. Tel: (031) 21 2783. Open Mon–Fri 0900–1730, Sat 0900–1630. Upbeat, colourful establishment celebrating the talents of local homeware designers.

Essenwood Craft Market

Essenwood Park, Essenwood Rd, the Berea. Tel: (031) 28 9916. Open Sat 0900–1400. Arts and crafts stalls in a tranquil park, plus tea garden and live music.

NSA Arts Gallery

166 Bulwer Rd, Glenwood. Tel: (031) 22 3686. Open Tue–Fri 0900–1700, Sat 0900–1600, Sun 1000–1400. The shop here is packed with fabulous locally-crafted wares; visit, too, for cutting-edge exhibitions and a café serving the best cheesecake in town.

Popatlall Kara

201 Grey St, City Centre. Tel: (031) 305 6881. Open Mon–Fri 0800–1700, Sat 0800–1300, Sun 1000–1500. Crammed with Indian delights, from saris in peacock colours to brightly-coloured kitsch.

What to buy

Don't miss the excellent **Ardmore Ceramic Art Studio** if you visit Champagne Castle in the Drakensberg – these highly original designs have won several awards. *Open daily 0900–1600. Tel: (036) 468 1314. Signposted from the R600, between the Nest Hotel and the Drakensberg Sun.*

Open-air art galleries of the Drakensberg

*South Africa's earliest inhabitants were the **San** peoples, diminutive, light-skinned hunter-gatherers who until the arrival of the white man in the 19th century had roamed the interior relatively undisturbed for generations – indeed, for some 40,000 years. As their traditional hunting grounds were annexed for farmland and vast herds of game were cut down by the settlers' guns, the San launched fierce retaliatory raids – to no avail. Their bows and arrows were no match for bullets, and they were simply hunted like vermin until they were more or less extinct.*

Yet the legacy they left was a rich one. Scattered throughout the country are more than 15,000 rock paintings and

engravings, ranging in age from about 20,000 years to about 100 years old. Some of the most vivid and detailed art is in the **Drakensberg**, where over 600 sites have been found – the oldest dating back some 800 years.

When you visit, though, bear in mind that San art isn't always a naturalistic depiction of everyday life. Many paintings stem from a supernatural view of the world – images of animals, for example, were regarded as miniature storehouses of the beasts' occult powers, and potent things in themselves.

Tapping into this power, it was believed, made contact with the spirit world possible. Images of eland are especially common, for as the largest of the African antelopes, these were thought to have a special link with the Godhead.

Another popular theme is trance-dancing, the method used by clan shamans to activate their supernatural powers and enter the spirit world. Paintings show women clapping and men dancing before an extraordinary figure, half-animal, half-human – the shaman, merging with his animal powers. Other common trance side effects, such as nosebleeds, are clearly expressed.

The three major Drakensberg sites are **Game Pass Shelter** in the Southern Berg's **Kamberg Reserve** (beautifully painted figures in trance states and eland); **Main Caves** at **Giant's Castle** (over 500 images); and **Battle Cave at Injasuti**, a large cave with many splendid paintings, some of which are thought to depict a clash between shamans in trance states and evil spirits.

Across the Interior

This epic route will appeal to lovers of space and silence, who find beauty in big skies and untamed, empty landscapes. Heading west from the lonely battlefields of KwaZulu-Natal and the Free State to bleak Namaqualand and the red Kalahari, it's a magnificent way to experience the scenic variety – and sheer vastness – of this remarkable land.

*Tourist information: **The Free State: Bloemfontein Tourist Information**: Tourist Centre, 60 Park Rd, Willows. Tel: (051) 405 8489. Open Mon–Fri 0800–1615, Sat 0800–1200. **The Northern Cape: Diamantveld Regional Tourist Information Centre**: 121 Bultfontein St, Kimberley. Tel: (053) 832 7298. Website: www.kimberley-africa.com. Open Mon–Fri 0800–1700, Sat 0830–1230.*

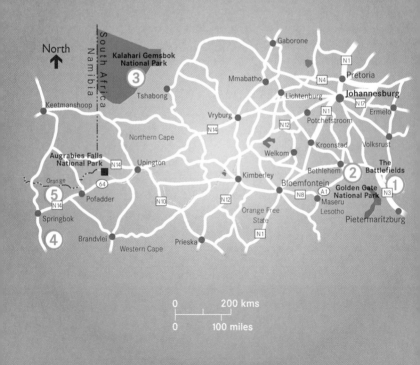

① The Battlefields

The huge, rolling plains of KwaZulu-Natal's northwestern corner were a crucible for much bloody conflict in the late 19th century, with the Zulus fighting the Boer and British forces who had invaded their land, and the latter fighting each other. Visit with a good guide to see this ghost-filled region transformed into a poignant storybook. **Pages 96–97**

② The Free State

When the Boers trekked away from British rule at the Cape in 1836, they crossed the Orange River to find fertile prairies, teeming with game. Farmers have tamed the prairies now, and hunters have long since seen off the game, but visitors still come to unwind in the sleepy Boer villages, and to hike and ride in the sandstone mountains marking the Lesotho border. **Pages 98–99**

③ The Kalahari Desert

It takes long hours of driving down dusty, monotonous roads and through miles of sweltering scrub to reach the Kalahari – definitely something of an endurance test. Yet the outstanding Kalahari Gemsbok National Park is well worth the trouble it takes to get here, offering great game-viewing in a magnificent wide-open, semi-desert setting. **Pages 100–101**

④ Namaqualand's spring flowers

Each spring, this stony region – monochromatic for most of the year – bursts out into an incredible array of brightly-coloured wildflowers. It's one of South Africa's most astonishing natural spectacles. **Pages 102–103**

⑤ Orange River Rafting

Peace and tranquility are what you'll experience as you raft down the big, easy waters of the Orange in northern Namaqualand, past cliffs and farmland and into the spectacular mountain desert of the Richtersveld. **Page 103**

Flower power

Because the distances in **Namaqualand** are so great, spring wild flower trips need to be carefully planned. Contact local tourist information offices or the **Flower Hotline** (*tel: (021) 418 3705*) day by day before you travel to find out where the best displays are, and remember that the flowers open at about 1000 every morning, closing up again around 1600.

95

The battlefield route

Simunye Zulu Lodge

Tel: (035) 45 3111. Overnight guests only. Accommodation: ££. Strike inland on the R34 from the industrial centre of Empangeni (173km north of Durban on the N2), then turn right onto the D256 just before Melmoth.

A good place to begin your journey is at KwaZulu-Natal's Simunye Zulu Lodge which borders a working *kraal*. Here, you can hear tales of battles with the British from a Zulu perspective, sample traditional food, drink and dancing, and receive a reasonably unsanitised introduction to Zulu history and culture first-hand. Accommodation's either in cottages at the lodge, or beehive village huts.

Ondini Historical Reserve

Open Mon–Fri 0800–1600, Sat–Sun 0900–1600. Admission: £. Book accommodation through the Clerk, KwaZulu-Natal Monuments Council, PO Box 523, Ulundi 3838, tel: (0358) 702050.

Some 42km north of Melmoth lies **Ulundi**, the functional former capital of the 'homeland' of KwaZulu. Outside town, heading north on the R66, a signposted gravel turn-off to the right takes you to the Ondini Historical Reserve, complete with *isigodlo* – a detailed reconstruction of King Cetshwayo's palace, burned to the ground by the British after the Battle of Ulundi in 1879. Two museums fill in background detail, while accommodation's available in beehive huts.

Isandlwana

Retracing your route south, turn right onto the R68 at the T-junction just outside Melmoth. A signposted turn-off to the left between Babanango and Nqutu brings you to the battlefield of Isandlwana where, beneath a sinister, sphinx-like hill, cairns of white stones mark the graves of British soldiers of the 24th Regiment. Over 1300 troops died here in January 1879 at the hands of a 25,000-strong Zulu *impi* (army), one of the most catastrophic defeats in British colonial history.

Gandhi

Outside Ladysmith's Vishnu Temple in Forbes Street stands a statue of Gandhi, who worked here as a stretcher-bearer with the British army during the Boer War.

Rorke's Drift

Back on the R68, a turn-off just 7km north of Nqutu leads left to Rorke's Drift, where (as viewers of the 1964 epic, *Zulu*, will recall) on that same fateful January day, 139 British soldiers holed up in a tiny mission station here valiantly held off some 4000 Zulus – an heroic 12-hour defence which earned them an unprecedented 11 Victoria Crosses. An absorbing little museum (*tel: (034) 642 1627; open daily 0800–1700; free*) at the site gives a full account of events, making this the best battlefield to visit if you don't have a guide.

Dundee

The best place for more background information on both the Zulu and Anglo-Boer Wars is the coal-mining centre of Dundee, reached via a 32km drive west from the Rorke's Drift turn-off on the R68. Here you'll find the excellent **Talana Museum** (*tel: (341) 22654; open Mon–Fri 0800–1600, Sat 1000–1600, Sun 1200–1600; admission: £*) just 2km outside town on the R33 to Vryheid, occupying a series of historic buildings on the site of the Boer War's first major battle in 1899.

Ladysmith

Now head west along the R68 and turn left at the T-junction onto the N11, following signs to the old Voortrekker town of Ladysmith (61km). In 1899, the British were besieged by Boer forces here for a terrible 118 days – a travail which the **Ladysmith Siege Museum** recounts in graphic detail (*cnr Queen and Murchison Sts; tel: (036) 637 2231; open Mon–Fri 0800–1600, Sat 0900–1300; admission: £*).

The Eastern Highlands

The mountainous countryside skirting the Free State's Lesotho border is much the most dramatic this fertile farming region has to offer. The beautiful 250km Highlands Route from Harrismith to Ladybrand via Ficksburg and Clocolan shows it at its best, with the smoky-blue Maluti Mountains on one side, rolling wheatfields on the other and huge skies above; this is star-in-your-own-road-movie country par excellence.

Qwaqwa National Park

Open daily. To book the Sentinel Trail, tel: (058) 713 4191. Free.

From Harrismith, it's 47km along the tarred R712 to flyblown **Phuthadijhaba**, gateway to the Qwaqwa National Park. Covering some 30,000 hectares of unspoiled mountain country, the park's highlight is the popular **Sentinel Trail**, the easiest route up the mighty Drakensberg plateau and the 3282m **Mont-aux-Sources** peak. Follow signs from town south to the **Witsieshoek Mountain Inn**, but turn left for the **Sentinel Car Park** after about 15km, where the road forks. From here, it's a 3km walk to the foot of Mont-aux-Sources, where a handy 30m-high chain-ladder leaves you within reach of the summit and its panoramic views – just three hours after you left the car park.

Basotho Cultural Village

Tel: (058) 721 0300. Open Mon–Fri 0900–1630, Sat–Sun 0900–1700. Free, but small fee for museum, trails, horse-rides and accommodation.

Under apartheid, Qwaqwa was the 'independent homeland' of the South Sotho peoples, and if you'd like a glimpse of their traditional way of life the Basotho Cultural Village (a signposted 10km detour from Phuthadijhaba) is happy to oblige. On the hokey but fun half-hour tour you can sip home-brewed beer, meet the chief and view beautifully decorated traditional huts, some of which date back to the

16th century. Most interesting of all, though, is the two-hour **Matlakeng Herbal Trail**, where a traditional healer gives an introduction to plants used in Sotho medicine.

Golden Gate National Park

30km west of Phuthadijhaba on the R712. Tel: (058) 255 0012. Open daily. Free. Book accommodation through the National Parks Board, PO Box 7400, Roggebaai, Cape Town 8012, tel: (021) 22 2810; or PO Box 787, Pretoria 0001, tel: (012) 343 1991.

Wind and rain have carved fantastic sculptures from the honey- and copper-coloured sandstone crags of the Golden Gate National Park, creating some outstanding drives and trails. Pick of the walks is the two-day, 31km circular **Rhebok Hiking Trail** through wild flower-sprinkled grasslands and stunning mountain scenery, where you might see black eagle and bearded vultures. Two rest-camps offer chalets, rondavels and a campsite.

Clarens

15km west of Golden Gate along the R712.

Despite the Free State's dour reputation for red-neck conservatism, several of its prettiest hamlets have been 'discovered' by city artists and bohemians, drawn by the low crime rates, lovely scenery and authentic village life. Cupped in a glen beneath stripy sandstone cliffs, tranquil Clarens is one of the nicest along this route: galleries and craft shops dot its willow-lined streets, while many of the old Voortrekker cottages now house artists' studios and B&Bs. It's a fine base for exploring the local horse-riding and hiking trails and trout-fishing opportunities.

Boer connection

Like the rest of the Free State, Clarens has strong Boer roots. It's named after the Swiss town where Boer leader Paul Kruger died in 1904.

Into the Kalahari

Kimberley

Lying as it does on a major crossroads, dusty **Kimberley** (293km from Ladybrand on the N8) is an obvious starting-point for this route west. The town is a dowdy shadow of its turn-of-the-century heyday, although the 365m-deep **Big Hole** is still compelling. Between 1871 and 1914, when excavation finally ended, it yielded nearly three tons of diamonds – dug by hand from the sticky grey ground. It's reached from the open-air **Mine Museum** (*Tucker St; open daily 0800–1800; admission: £*), an imaginative partial reconstruction of the original 'rush town', spread along the crater's western edge.

Witsand Nature Reserve

Tel: (053) 313 1061/2. Open daily 0800–1800. Admission: £.

Witsand Nature Reserve, 279km further west in the shadow of the Langberg Mountains, makes a tranquil introduction to the scrub-dotted, semi-desert Kalahari landscape. It's also home to a freakish 9km patch of albino dunes, the so-called 'roaring sands'. Any disturbance to the southernmost fringes of these dunes – especially in hot, dry weather – creates an extraordinary bass groaning sound that has to be heard to be believed. To get here, follow the R64 through **Griquatown** and take the signposted turning right just before Volop; it's another 45km to the gates, on gravel. Accommodation ranges from comfortable thatched chalets to a campsite.

> " We climbed on to the roofs of our Land Rovers and looked further into that remote world sealed with red sand, and spread out as still as the water of a locked ocean. "
>
> **Laurens van der Post, *The Lost World of the Kalahari*, London 1958**

Kalahari-Gemsbok National Park

Tel: (054) 561 0021. Open daily 0700–1800 (but hours vary slightly every month). Admission: £. Book accommodation through the National Parks Board, PO Box 7400, Roggebaai, Cape Town 8012, tel: (021) 22 2810; or PO Box 787, Pretoria 0001, tel: (012) 343 1991.

Some 205km northwest along the N10 lies the prosperous farming town of **Upington**, your last chance to stock up on essentials before tackling the final sweltering 288km north

(60km on gravel) to the Kalahari-Gemsbok National Park. This enormous (3.6 million-hectare) stretch of rust-coloured dunes and cracked salt-pans, shimmering in the desert heat, is one of the world's best places to see cheetah – the park's dry riverbeds give them plenty of hunting space. Other carnivores such as lion, bat-eared fox and both brown and spotted hyena are abundant, while the magnificent range of raptors includes martial and tawny eagle, and eagle owl.

Twee Rivieren is the closest camp to the entrance, and therefore the busiest. **Mata Mata** (120km further north) and Nossob (160km) are more basic, but their isolated settings lend them a rather romantic desert atmosphere.

Augrabies Falls National Park

Tel: (054) 451 0050. Open daily Apr–Sept 0630–2200, Oct–Mar 0600–2200. Admission: £. Book accommodation through the National Parks Board, PO Box 7400, Roggebaai, Cape Town 8012, tel: (021) 22 2810; or PO Box 787, Pretoria 0001, tel: (012) 343 1991.

The Augrabies Falls National Park is an easy day trip from Upington – it's 129km west along the N14, hugging the lush banks of the mighty Orange River. The main attraction here is an awesome waterfall where the Orange thunders 56m down into a deep gorge, sending up vast sheets of spray in an echoing roar. Game drives through the park's lunar-landscape scenery offer the chance to see giraffe and various small antelope; there's also a rest-camp with self-catering chalets.

Namaqualand

As every South African schoolchild knows, the desolate slice of coast wedged between Namibia and the Western Cape bursts into brilliant colour for a few weeks every spring (Sept–Oct), when the wild flowers bloom. The sight is one of the country's most dazzling natural attractions, drawing floods of visitors from around the globe.

Springbok

374km west of Upington on the N14, and 550km from Cape Town.

Set amidst hills thickly carpeted with flowers in season, Springbok, Namaqualand's capital makes a good base for exploring. **Goegap Nature Reserve** (*15km southeast of town on the R355; tel: (0251) 21880; open daily 0800–1600; admission: £*) is a good place to start – it incorporates the excellent **Hester Malan Wild Flower Garden**, at its most spectacular in spring, but still worth visiting whatever the season for its hiking and mountain-biking trails through the aloes and succulents. Accommodation is in two self-catering chalets.

Kamieskroon and Garies

Heading south, the bleak boulder-mountain country surrounding the villages of Kamieskroon and Garies on the N7 is one of the most rewarding flower regions. Vygies (pink, blue and scarlet mesembryanthemums) cover the rocky slopes, while you'll also see extensive fields of orange gousblom daisies, and – towards the end of the season – the beautiful metre-high bulbinella. Don't miss the ever-reliable **Skilpad Wildflower Reserve** (*tel: (027) 672 1614; open only in flower season 0800–1700; admission: £*), well signposted just 7km west of Kamieskroon. As it enjoys a slightly higher rainfall than the surrounding areas, displays are often superb even in a disappointing season.

Tip

As Namaqualand's spring wild flowers turn to face the sun, drive westwards in the morning, and eastwards in the afternoon.

Richtersveld National Park

Tel: (0256) 831 1506. Open daily 0800–1600. Admission: £. Book accommodation through the National Parks Board, PO Box 7400, Roggebaai, Cape Town 8012, tel: (021) 22 2810; or PO Box 787, Pretoria 0001, tel: (012) 343 1991.

Some 330km north of Springbok via Port Nolloth and Alexander Bay, the Richtersveld National Park is one of South Africa's remotest reserves. No big game roams this heat-seared mountainscape (in summer, daytime temperatures often reach 50°C (112°F)) but you'll see plenty of small antelope such as klipspringer, along with indigenous desert plants like the weird *halfmens* – a tall, spiny succulent topped with a clump of Medusa-like leaves. Exploring the Richterveld's bleak lunar peaks and rocks is undoubtedly an adventure, as long as you don't mind roughing it – water is scarce, the campsites have no facilities and you must have a 4WD. The small HQ at **Sendelingsdrift** has two basic chalets.

One of the nicest – and, perhaps, most realistic – ways to explore the Richtersveld is on a guided canoeing trip down the **Orange River**. Where it uncoils like a fat brown serpent along the Namaqualand border, the river's mostly broad and sluggish, offering leisurely paddling where you can gaze at the bone-dry hills beyond the fertile river bank, and enjoy the rich birdlife. There are a few good rapids, too, so at least you can swap bruising tales around the campfire at night. Reputable operators, such as the Cape Town-based **Felix Unite River Adventures** (*tel: (021) 683 6433; ££*) offer four- to six-day trips from Noordoewer into the national park, with camps set up *en route*.

103

Eating and drinking

As you might expect, South Africa's small inland towns and dorps are hardly oversubscribed with gourmet outlets – indeed, the ubiquitous Wimpy chain of burger bars may well prove to be your mainstay as you explore this route.

If you're lucky, you may find homely restaurants in the Northern Cape dishing up unusual regional specialities like *kambro* (a potato-like tuber, traditionally cooked with ginger, wild fennel and honey), or Kalahari truffles. In the Free State, slow-roasted *blesbok* is the dish to look out for.

Tea shops and bars

The Battlefields

Babanango: Stan's Pub

Babanango Hotel, 16 Justice St. Tel: (0358) 35 0029. Open daily 0900–late. £. Hung with memorabilia from the 1979 film, *Zulu Dawn*, this atmospheric little pub's hospitable reputation has spread far and wide.

Dundee: Miners' Rest Tea Shop

Talana Museum, 2km north of town on the R33. Tel: (341) 22654. Open Mon–Fri 0800–1600, Sat 1000–1600, Sun 1200–1600. £. Set in a pretty old cottage shaded by blue gums, this is a pleasant place for a cup of tea and a snack.

The Free State

Clarens: Maluti Mountain Lodge

Steil St, signposted off the R712 to Bethlehem. Tel: (058) 256 1422. Open daily 1000–late. £. Cosy, graffiti-covered hotel pub where you could find yourself swapping stories with farmers, tourists, artists and trout fishermen alike.

The Kalahari

Upington: Scotty's Bar

Oasis Protea Lodge, 24 Schröder St. Tel: (054) 331 1125. Open daily 1000–late. £. Pleasant local hangout in this centrally situated business hotel; gets very lively at weekends.

Namaqualand

Kamieskroon: Kamieskroon Hotel

Old National Rd. Tel: (027) 672 1614. Open daily 1000–late. £. Friendly country pub.

Restaurants

The Battlefields

Ladysmith:
The Royal Hotel

140 Murchison St. Tel: (036) 637 2176. Closed Sun. £££. This historic building sheltered the local élite during the siege of 1899–1900, and was regularly shelled by the Boers. Now houses three restaurants, including **Swainson's**, the smartest place to eat in town. International cuisine.

The Free State

Clarens: Street Caffé [sic]

Main St. Tel: (058) 256 1561. Open daily lunch and dinner. £. Pizzas, toasted sandwiches, grills and homemade cakes, served on a shady veranda.

Ladybrand:
Cranberry Cottage

37 Beeton St. Tel: (05191) 2290. Open daily lunch and dinner. ££. Pretty Victorian guesthouse offering elegant South African meals (good vegetarian options) in chintzy surroundings.

The Kalahari

Upington: Le Must

11 Schröder St. Tel: (054) 332 5779. Open Mon–Fri lunch and dinner; Sat dinner only. ££. A real find. Imaginative cooking with a Provençale touch.

Namaqualand

Springbok: Springbok Lodge & Restaurant

Cnr Voortrekker and Keerom Rds. Tel: (0251) 21321. Open daily lunch and dinner. £. Local institution offering plain, hearty grub. Good value, though, and there's always a chance of interesting characters passing through.

What to try

Wherever you are in the Free State, keep an eye out for roadside farm stalls stocking such Afrikaner delicacies as *biltong* (strips of dried, cured meat), *tsammakonfyt* (melon jam), *beskuit* (rusks – for dipping in coffee) and heavenly *melktert* (nutmeg-spiced custard tart).

What to buy

The Zulu beadwork you'll see for sale as you travel through the Battlefields region may have a message attached. Traditionally, white beads were used to signify love and purity, blue faithfulness, and red longing; stitched together, these produced a poignant love letter in jewellery form.

Theatre, performance and cinema

The Battlefields: the best guide to the Anglo-Zulu battle sites of Rorke's Drift and Isandlwana – and, some say, the best one-man show in South Africa – is **David Rattray**, who runs a small lodge near the sites. Highly recommended. **Fugitive's Drift Lodge**: *PO Box 3016, Rorke's Drift. Tel: (03425) 843.*

Shopping

The Battlefields

Rorke's Drift Battlefield: Evangelical Lutheran Church Arts and Crafts Centre

Tel: (03425) 627. Open Mon–Fri 0800–1630, Sat 1000–1500. Zulu craftsmen and women have been producing award-winning karakul-wool rugs, tapestries, pottery and hand-printed fabrics for more than 30 years on this evocative site.

The Free State

Clarens: Di Mezza & De Jager Trading Store

Sias Oosthuizen St. Tel: (058) 256 1313. Open Mon–Fri 0800–1300, 1400–1700, Sat 0800–1200. Old-fashioned general dealer with a fine selection of pure-wool blankets in bright designs, worn like cloaks by the local Basotho.

Rooikat Gallery

Market St North. Tel: (058) 256 1558. By appointment only. If hunting knives are your thing, local craftsman Roy Clark makes particularly fine ones, with bone or polished wood handles. His wife sells her pottery here, too.

The Northern Cape

Kimberley: Art Market

Harry Oppenheimer Gardens. Tel: (0531) 842 0225. Open last Sat of the month 0800–1300. Stalls sell handcrafts, plus art and flea market goodies. Live entertainment includes singers and musicians.

Richtersveld National Park

Tel: (0256) 831 1506. Open daily 0800–1600. The rest-camp here stocks distinctive, unusual crafts produced by the local Nama people, from traditional reed mats to textile designs based on ancient rock engravings and indigenous desert flora.

All that glitters . . .

More diamonds have come out of Kimberley than any other city in the world – and as the world knows, diamonds remain one of the mainstays of the South African economy. It all began in 1871, when diamond deposits found on a hillock owned by a certain pair of brothers named De Beer led to a feverish 'rush', and the hasty erection of an overcrowded, unsanitary shanty-town born of desperation and greed. That hillock

is now the Big Hole, and Kimberley a prosperous modern town, its higgledy-piggledy web of roads the only topographic reminder of a chaotic past.

Entrepreneur **Cecil Rhodes** – as politically ruthless as he was financially savvy – was the man who did most to organise the fledgling industry. Sent out to South Africa as a sickly teenager in 1871, within a decade he had founded De Beers Consolidated; by 1889 it had become the world's pre-eminent mining-house, a position it still holds today.

Fittingly, perhaps, De Beer's **Bultfontein** diggings just outside Kimberley is the only place in the world where you can take an underground tour of an operational diamond mine. It's not for the faint-hearted, or the remotely claustrophobic, though: after a safety talk and a brief audiovisual presentation,

you're handed your miner's gear (overalls, hard hat, a torch and emergency oxygen pack), ushered into the shaft lift and sunk all the way down into the belly of the earth – or, to be more precise, a depth of 825m.

Once underground, amidst the roar of turbines and in the sweltering heat, you're guided round the chambers where the blue-tinged, diamond-rich Kimberlite is blasted, scooped out into trolleys and then hauled up to the surface to be sieved. Spot one of the glittering rocks yourself (although it's highly unlikely) and De Beers will give you 20 per cent of its value, which according to them is a better deal than you would get on the black market. It's your call.
Tel: (053) 842 1321. By appointment only; no children under 16. Admission: £.

Gauteng

Gold was the catalyst which brought Gauteng ('Place of Gold' in Sotho) into being, transforming it into the pulsating heart of South Africa's economic life. It's one of the world's wealthiest

nuggets of land, home to fast-paced
Johannesburg – and a string of townships
as vast as they are poor. 'Place of Contrasts'
would be just as good a name.

111

BEST OF
Gauteng

Tourist information: **Tourism Johannesburg**: *Sandown Centre, cnr Rivonia Rd and Maude St, Sandown. Tel: (011) 784 1354. Open Mon–Fri 0830–1630, Sat 0900–1800, Sun 0900–1200.* **Pretoria Tourism**: *Tourist Rendezvous Travel Centre, cnr Vermeulen and Prinsloo Sts. Tel: (012) 308 8909. Open Mon–Fri 0800–1545.*

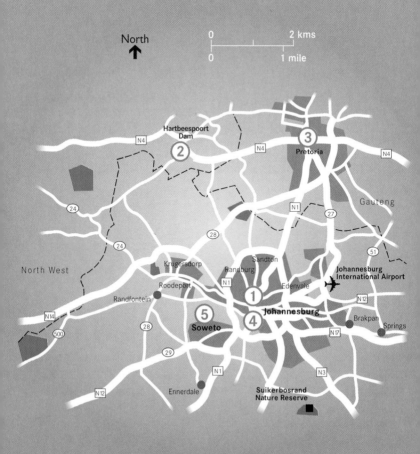

① African Manhattan

Crime-ridden, polluted, grimly industrial: e'Goli, the City of Gold, is all these things. Yet those who stay and explore are usually pleasantly surprised: Jo'burg has a high-voltage, patently African urban buzz like no other in the country, while its feisty, hard-nosed spirit keeps it at the cutting edge of art and culture as well as finance. **Pages 114–117, 124–125**

② The Magaliesberg

The ochre ridges of this Highveld mountain range are a favourite retreat for stressed-out Gautengers, who come to hike its crags and gorges and fish and swim in the huge Hartbeespoort Dam. **Page 119**

③ Pretoria

Smaller and prettier than Johannesburg, and safer, too, the country's administrative capital makes a good base for exploring Gauteng. Not only do jacarandas blossom here, this former apartheid bastion now hosts some of the hippest Afro-chic nightlife around, with a thriving gay scene. **Pages 120–121, 124**

④ Golden City nightlife

You'll find South Africa's best and most sophisticated nightlife in Johannesburg, and the most varied. Thanks to its position at the centre of the local music scene, most of the country's top bands are based here, with key East, West and Central African groups gigging regularly, too. **Pages 126–127**

⑤ Soweto

It may seem bizarre to treat it as a tourist attraction, but a guided tour is much the safest and most practical way to get a glimpse of South Africa's most famous township. **Pages 126–127**

Getting around

Johannesburg: nobody walks anywhere here, except in the northern suburbs – and even then, only by day. Unless you're familiar with the city, the very real risk of car-jacking means driving is not a good idea, but, if you do decide to hire a car, make sure the doors are locked and the windows closed as you drive, especially at traffic lights.

Minibus 'black taxis' are a definite no-no, as long-standing taxi wars over territory mean ranks have been the site of random shootings.

Trains: Johannesburg's rail network also has a dodgy reputation, safety-wise, and in any case offers very limited services.

Taxis: first choice for safety is hotel transport, or official taxis, which you have to book by appointment – they can't be flagged down on the street. Reliable operators include **Sabto** (*tel: (011) 390 1502*) and **Village Cabs** (*tel: (011) 887 2207*).

Buses: the municipal bus service offers a fairly reliable between the centre and the suburbs during the day, but not at night – most stop running around 1830. Weekend services are extremely sporadic. Timetables are available at the Tourism Johannesburg office, or the main terminus in Van Der Bijl Square in the city centre (*tel: (011) 403 4300*).

Pretoria: local buses run between the city centre and the suburbs. Timetables are available from the tourist information office.

Taxis: reliable operators include **Baby Cabs** (*tel: (012) 324 6222*) and **Cool Cats** (*tel: (012) 321 1999/1012*).

Johannesburg:
art and culture

As you explore Jo'burg's galleries and museums, keep an eye out, too, for the little pockets of pleasure that transform this avowedly ugly heart of the nation: the monumental lion-coloured mine-dumps; the mad turrets of a Randlord's mansion, high on a ridge; steam rising off streets carpeted in jacaranda blossom after a summer storm.

Downtown Jo'burg is a colourful jumble of skyscrapers towering over Indian bazaars and African muti (medicine) shops, where office workers rub shoulders with hawkers, beggars and amaGents – well-heeled wide boys. It's also one of the city's most crime-ridden areas, so be extra alert as you travel to the sprawling **Newtown Cultural Precinct**, a cluster of warehouses just west of the city centre, now converted into venues for experimental theatre, galleries and museums.

MuseuMAfrikA

121 Bree St. Tel: (011) 833 5624. Open Tue–Sun 0900–1700. Admission: £, free Sun. From the M1 North or South, take the Smit St off-ramp.

Best of all is MuseuMAfrikA, with its innovative displays on township life and apartheid politics – a fine place to get a handle on the country's rapidly changing cultural focus. Heading east down Bree St, **Joubert Park** is Jo'burg's only inner-city green space, although it's definitely not a place to linger.

Johannesburg Art Gallery

Klein St, Joubert Park. Tel: (011) 725 3130. Open Tue–Sun 1000–1700. Admission: £.

Do, however, visit the Johannesburg Art Gallery, housed in a stately Lutyens-designed building on the park's southern border. Post-apartheid, the gallery's small but perfectly formed collection of European works by the likes of **Rodin** and **Picasso** has been augmented by an excellent selection of black art and artefacts, including several marvellous pieces by the Venda shaman-sculptor, **Jackson Hlungwane**.

Gertrude Posel Gallery

Senate House, Jorissen St, University of the Witwatersrand. Tel: (011) 716 3632. Open Tue–Fri 1000–1600, Sat by appointment. Free.

Known colloquially as 'Wits', Jo'burg's university campus lies just northwest of the city centre in Braamfontein. It's home to the rewarding Gertrude Posel Gallery, whose impressive permanent collections focus on vanishing traditional African art forms from drums to beadwork, as well as contemporary works.

Parktown

North of the campus, beyond Empire Rd, posh Parktown – the city's oldest élite suburb – perches on a leafy ridge. The **Parktown & Westcliff Heritage Trust** (*Northwards, Rockridge Rd; tel: (011) 482 3349; open Mon–Fri 0900–1300; £*)

offer entertaining walking tours round the area's opulent turn-of-the-century mansions (many built by **Herbert Baker**), led by guides in full Edwardian dress.

115

Melville Koppies Nature Reserve

Judith Rd, Emmerentia. Tel: (011) 782 7064. Open May–Sept every third Sun of the month. Free. Take Empire Rd heading north through Barry Herzog Ave, and follow the signs.

> " . . . the whole crest of the Rand ridge was fringed with factory chimneys . . . I might have been looking from a distance at Oldham. "
>
> **The young war correspondent Winston Churchill, 1900**

Covered in indigenous scrub and veld flowers, the Melville Koppies Nature Reserve is a tranquil oasis within sight of downtown's skyscrapers. These rocky outcrops are the southernmost section of the much larger Jan Van Riebeeck Park; they also contain both Stone and Iron Age ruins.

Johannesburg: street markets and malls

Since the start of the 1990s, city flea markets have been flooded with traders bringing in wares from East, West and Central Africa, providing sweet pickings as far as ethnic crafts are concerned, and some excellent people-watching opportunities, too. Goods are much cheaper than in the curio shops, and bargaining can bring the price down further.

Market Theatre

Cnr Bree and Wolhuter Sts, Newtown. Tel: (011) 832 1641. Open Sat 0900–1600.

The city's original flea market still takes place every Saturday outside the Market Theatre in downtown Jo'burg (next door to the Newtown Precinct), where a crowded, colourful sprawl of 350-odd stalls sell everything from semiprecious stones to wirework and carved animal figures. While the square and theatre complex are patrolled by uniformed guards 24 hours a day (a depressing but commonplace feature of everyday life in e'Goli), the surrounding area is less safe. Take care.

Flea Market World

Cnr Ernest Oppenheimer Drive and Marcia St, Bruma Lake. Tel: (011) 786 0776. Open Tue–Fri 0930–1800, Sat 0830–1800, Sun 0900–1800.

Heading east from the city centre and out onto the airport road, Flea Market World at tatty **Bruma Lake** shopping complex is a chaotic buzz of people and traders. With over 600 stalls to choose from, the quality of craftwork is generally high – especially the carved wooden masks and sticks, and lengths of printed fabric from Zaire. Just don't let the rather moth-eaten troupes of 'traditional' Zulu dancers put you off your haggling.

Rooftop Market, Rosebank

Top Floor Parking Lot, Rosebank Mall, 50 Bath Rd.
Tel: (011) 442 4488. Open Sun 0930–1700.

Affluent **Rosebank**, just north of Houghton is where you'll find the excellent weekly Rooftop Market. Along with stalls flogging antiques, toys, health food, clothing and metalwork, there's a fabulous range of African artefacts, from the Ivory Coast's painted wooden figurines (pink-cheeked, pith-helmeted colonial administrators seem to be a favourite subject) to Nigerian and Ghanaian masks and fetishes. Traders also line Cradock Ave outside, between the mall and Mutual Square.

Organic Village Market, Bryanston

Michael Mount Waldorf School, Culross Rd, off Main Rd, Bryanston.
Tel: (011) 706 3671. Open Thur 0900–1300, Sat 0900–1400, moonlight markets every Tue nearest the full moon 0500–2100.

Heading still further north beyond Sandton, the rich hippy intelligentsia of leafy **Bryanston** keep Jo'burg's swankiest 'flea', the Organic Village Market, a fixture on the arts and crafts map. Amidst the fine organic produce, the handmade clothing (beware – batik trouser alert) and those ubiquitous beeswax candles are some top-quality crafts, from ceramics and glassware to funky jewellery.

Harbour Market, Randburg

Randburg Waterfront, Republic Rd. Tel: (011) 886 0208.
Open Tue–Sun 1000–1700.

Just west of Bryanston off the R71 lies dismally suburban **Randburg**, home to the vast Waterfront shopping-and-leisure complex, built round an artificial lake. Best feature is the busy Harbour Market, where you can watch artisans at work and buy their wares – tapestries, pottery, furniture and African artefacts.

Parktown Prawn

Sobering crime statistics aside, what really strikes fear into Jo'burger's hearts is a sighting of the legendary Parktown Prawn in the living room. This repellent, rank-smelling creature – a member of the cockroach family – can grow up to 7.5cm long.

Around Johannesburg

Witwatersrand National Botanic Garden

Malcolm Rd, Poortview, Roodepoort. Tel: (011) 958 1750.
Open daily 0800–1700. Admission: £.

For a glimpse of South Africa's most industrialised province
as it was before the arrival of the gold-diggers, head
west out of town on the R47 to **Roodepoort**'s beautiful
Witwatersrand National Botanic Garden. An entire slab of
mountainside forms the backdrop for the park's 600 species
of Highveld aloes, cycads and shrubs – although top billing
goes to the noble pair of rare black eagles nesting on the
cliff-face, near a 70m waterfall.

Suikerbosrand Nature Reserve

Tel: (011) 904 3930. Open Mon–Fri 0715–1600, Sat–Sun 0700–1700.
Admission: £. Take the N3 from Jo'burg and then turn right onto the R550,
following the signs.

Further afield, some 40km south of the city, the Suikerbosrand
Nature Reserve is a pristine stretch of 'High Country' grassland,
scattered with rocky ridges and tree-filled gorges. Best bet
for day visitors is the two-hour, 4.5km **Cheetah Interpretive
Trail** that starts and ends at the Diepkloof Visitor's Centre –
you could spot eland, kudu and baboon as well as zebra.

Sterkfontein Caves

Tel: (011) 956 6342. Open Tue–Sun 0900–1600.
Guided tours every 30 mins. Admission: £. Take
the R47 west out of Jo'burg through Muldersdrift,
turning right at the R563 junction and following
the signs.

An unprepossessing hillock
on the outskirts of dreary
Krugersdorp, 40km northwest of
Jo'burg, contains the dramatic
Sterkfontein Caves, Gauteng's
oldest archaeological site. Pre-
human primates lived here over
three million years ago, claim
anthropologists, but that's not

the only reason to visit. Underground water has dissolved the dolomitic rock to create gargantuan chambers, and an equally large, Stygian lake.

Magaliesberg

Northwest of Krugersdorp, bordering the imaginatively-named North-West Province, lies the craggy spine of the Magaliesberg. This small but beautiful mountain range is a handy bolthole for stressed-out Jo'burgers, who go yachting and water-skiing on the huge **Hartbeespoort Dam** here and stay in the leafy holiday resorts dotting its shores. The **Magaliesberg Express** steam train offers pleasant day trips to the range – a soothing three-hour journey each way through rolling yellow grasslands, with lunch at the Magaliesburg Country Hotel. *Tel: (011) 888 1154. Trips twice monthly, Sun only. Depart Johannesburg Station 0845, return by 1745. Tickets: ££.*

Lesedi Cultural Village

174 Kalkheuwel, Pelindaba Rd, Broederstroom. Tel: (012) 205 1394. Daily performances 1130–1400, 1630–2100. Admission: ££. Take the R511 heading north to Hartbeespoort, then turn left onto the R512 at the Toll Plaza 4-way junction.

If the relentlessly Anglo-Saxon flavour of the Hartbeespoort holiday playground starts to pall, try a night at the Lesedi Cultural Village on the outskirts of tranquil **Broederstroom** Designed as a one-stop cultural experience, archetypal Xhosa, Zulu, Pedi and Sotho rural households have been recreated here in the rocky Magaliesberg hills. Contrived it undoubtedly is, but it's also good fun: spend time as the guest of one of the families who live and work here, enjoy an African feast and join in the traditional dancing and singing.

119

> " *The wealth of our mining industry is not so much due to the richness of gold as to the poorness of black wages.* "
>
> **Author Alan Paton, writing in the 1960s**

Pretoria

Until recently, South Africa's administrative capital (50km north of Johannesburg) suffered a severe image problem as a deeply conservative bastion of apartheid values. Now, however, a change of government and the arrival of an international diplomatic community has meant an energetic loosening of cultural collars all round.

Most historic sites, of course, still celebrate the city's staunchly Boer past. Take pedestrianised **Church Square** in the heart of the city, whose chief landmark is a looming statue of that dour old arch-Calvinist, Paul Kruger. **Strijdom Square**, a short walk east down Church St, is dominated by a giant bust of a more recent Volk hero – the white supremacist prime minister J G Strijdom.

Melrose House

275 Jacob Mare St. Tel: (012) 322 0420. Open Tue, Thur–Sat 1000–1700, Wed 1000–2000, Sun 1300–1800. Admission: £.

Much more uplifting is the lavishly gabled Melrose House, a 15-minute walk south down Van der Walt St past manicured **Burgers Park**. The Peace of Vereeniging – which ended the

Anglo-Boer War – was signed at this Victorian mansion in 1902; it's now a museum. There's a pleasant tea garden in the shady grounds, a conservatory filled with rampant ferns and a good museum shop selling antique clothing, too.

Pretoria Art Museum

Cnr Schoeman and Wessels Sts. Tel: (012) 344 1807.
Open Tue–Sat 1000–1700, Sun 1300–1800. Admission: £.

Back in the city centre, a short drive east down Schoeman St leads to the Pretoria Art Museum, a fine provincial gallery with work by South African artists (look out for paintings by the celebrated Afrikaner landscapist, **Pierneef**) and a handful of 17th-century Dutch masters.

Just north of the museum, splendidly positioned on the crest of a ridge, are the famous Herbert Baker-designed **Union Buildings**, seat of the South African government. This monumental red-sandstone landmark was the setting for Nelson Mandela's historic inauguration on 10 May 1994 – and while it's closed to the public, the beautifully kept terraced gardens command fabulous views.

UNISA Art Gallery

Fifth Floor, Theo van Wyk Building, B Block, Preller Rd. Tel: (012) 429 6255.
Open Mon–Fri 1000–1530, Sat 1430–1630. Free.

Drive south just beyond the city borders to find the UNISA Art Gallery, one of the best in town. Housed within the grounds of South Africa's largest correspondence university, its temporary exhibitions are always reliably cutting edge, and there's a rewarding permanent collection of works by up-and-coming local talent, too.

Correctional Services Museum

Prison Reserve, Potgieter St. Tel: (012) 314 1766. Open Tue–Fri 0900–1500, Sun 1000–1500. Admission: £.

Heading right out of town towards Johannesburg via Potgieter St and the R101, follow signs for **Pretoria Central Prison** – once one of apartheid's most hated symbols, now home to the distinctly odd Correctional Services Museum. It supposedly charts the development of South Africa's penal system (cue group shots of hatchet-faced warders) but far more intriguing are the displays of lethal-looking items secretly manufactured by the prisoners, from hollowed-out bibles concealing knives to razor-blade-laden shoes.

Eating and drinking

Cosmopolitan Johannesburg offers a huge variety of bars and restaurants, from good-value Portuguese and Italian outlets to upmarket eateries tucked safely away in the northern suburbs. Trendy Melville, just north of Braamfontein, is a vibrant district with a thriving café society, while Pretoria's Hatfield and Sunnyside suburbs are both reliably lively, too.

Cafés and bars

Johannesburg

Bob's Bar

76 Op de Bergen St, Troyeville. Tel: (011) 624 1894. Closed Tue. £. Once Jo'burg's hippest alternative hangout – but things have never been the same since Bob left. Still one of the most laid-back bars in town, though, with great views of Jo'burg's Manahattanesque skyline.

Radium Beer Hall

282 Louis Botha Ave, Orange Grove. Tel: (011) 728 3866. Closed Sun. £. Cheerful, mixed clientele, good music – and a great Portuguese menu, too.

The Full Stop

4a 7th Ave, Melville. Tel: (011) 726 3801. Open daily 0900–0200. £. Laid-back café, popular with writers, actors and poseurs carefully nursing epic hangovers behind dark glasses.

Pretoria

Café Riche

2 Church Square, City Centre. Tel: (012) 328 3173. Open daily 0600– midnight. ££. Pretoria's oldest café (now a national monument) dishes up hearty continental-style meals and snacks, along with excellent patisserie. A great brunch spot.

The Boere-Bar

The Yard, cnr Duncan and Prospect Sts, Hatfield. Tel: (012) 342 9950. Open daily 1000–midnight. £. This groovy nouveau-Afrikaner hangout with the heavily ironic décor gets the student vote. Live music at weekends.

Restaurants

Johannesburg

Anton Van Wouw

118 Siemert Rd, Doornfontein. Tel: (011) 402 7916. Open lunch Mon–Fri, dinner Mon–Sat. ££. Plush eaterie set in a revamped sculptor's studio, serving traditional Cape Dutch cuisine – hence plenty of game dishes, along with *bobotie*s and *bredie*s (spicy meat stews).

Cento

100 Langerman Drive, Kensington. Tel: (011) 622 7272. Open daily except Sat lunch. ££. Seafood dominates this Mediterranean-inspired menu, all fresh, all beautifully cooked. Plonk-free wine list, too.

Gramadoelas

Market Theatre Complex, Bree and Wolhuter Sts, Newtown. Tel: (011) 838 6960. Open lunch Tue–Sat, dinner Mon–Sat. ££. South African regional cooking at its best; try the sinful Malva Pudding. A magnet for visiting celebrities, too, including Hilary Clinton, Stevie Wonder and Catherine Deneuve.

Île de France

26 Cramerview Centre, 227 Main Rd, Bryanston. Tel: (011) 706 2837. Open daily except Sat lunch. £££. Don't be put off by the shopping-mall location – local foodies go into raptures over chef-owner Marc Guebert's fine Provençale cooking.

Ivaya

169 Oxford Rd, Mutual Square, Rosebank. Tel: (011) 327 1312. Open daily lunch and dinner. ££. Vibrant African décor, marvellous music and 'authentic Pan-African cuisine', from the Cape to Cairo. Try the *maafe* from Timbuktu: tender chicken in a nutty-flavoured sauce.

Pretoria

Gerhard Moerdyk

752 Park St, Arcadia Tel: (012) 344 4856. Open lunch Mon–Fri, dinner Mon–Sat. £££. Upmarket *boerekos* (Afrikaner cuisine) and an excellent wine list keep this elegant eatery packed with local diplomats and MPs.

The Odd Plate

262 Rhino St, Hennops Park Ext 2, Centurion. Tel: (012) 654 5203. Open lunch Wed–Fri, dinner Wed–Sat. ££. The training restaurant of South African-born Prue Leith's College of Food and Wine, set in gracious Lytton Manor House. Visit at weekends for the fine African fusion menu, cooked over open fires.

What to try

Chewy *mopani* worms – usually served in a spicy peri-peri sauce – are a feature of most traditional African menus. They're surprisingly tasty, too.

Clubs and nightlife

Johannesburg

The Bassline

7th St, Melville. Tel: (011) 482 6915. Open daily, bands start around 2100. ££. Great live jazz, blues and drumming; specialises in progressive jazz.

Carfax

39 Pim St, Newtown. Tel: (011) 834 9187. Open Mon–Fri 0900–1800, Sat 2130–0400. ££. Achingly hip performance space-cum-rave-venue: live music, DJs, multimedia, art . . .

Kippies Jazz International

Market Theatre, Bree St, Newtown. Tel: (011) 833 3316. Open daily. ££. All colours, all creeds – the only requirement is a love of jazz.

Roxy's Rhythm Bar

20 Main Rd, Melville. Tel: (011) 726 6019. Open Mon–Fri 1030–late, Sat 1500–late. ££. Top live rock venue and the best place to catch local superstars like the Springbok Nude Girls.

Pretoria

Crossroads Blues Bar

Upper Level, The Tramshed, cnr Schoeman and Van der Walt Sts. Tel: (012) 322 3263. Open daily. ££. Hip music venue, with live bands at weekends.

Yearlings

Cnr Rissik and Mears Sts, Sunnyside. Tel: (012) 341 9293. Open Fri, Sat 2100–late. ££. Pretoria's top gay club.

Theatre, performance and cinema

Johannesburg

Agfa Theatre on the Square

Sandton Square, Sandton. Tel: (011) 883 8606. Intimate venue staging all kinds of productions, from drama to musicals.

Hysterix Comedy Bar

Waterfront Complex, Randburg. Tel: (011) 787 0754. Closed Mon, Tue. Premier stand-up comedy venue.

The Market Theatre Complex

Newtown Cultural Precinct, Bree St and Wolhuter St, Newtown. Tel: (011) 836 1648. The home of anti-apartheid theatre in the 70s and 80s, now a thriving arts complex which includes three theatres.

Rosebank Mall Cinemas

Rosebank Mall, 50 Bath Rd. Tel: (011) 788 5530. Screens a good sprinkling of art-house and cult films along with blockbusters.

Pretoria

Pretoria State Theatre

320 Pretorius St, City Centre. Tel: (012) 322 1665. One of South Africa's leading performance venues.

Shopping

Johannesburg

Art Africa

62 Tyrone Ave, Parkview. Tel: (011) 486 2052. Open Mon–Fri 0900–1800, Sat 0900–1500. Crammed with ethnic artefacts from as far afield as Benin and Nigeria – there's something to suit all pockets here.

Congo Joe

4c Seventh St, Melville. Tel: (011) 726 4101. Open Mon–Fri 0900–1700, Sat 0900–1630. Highly collectable South African-made homeware, including Carol Boyd's striking pewter cutlery. Very Elle Deco.

Kim Sacks Gallery

153 Jan Smuts Ave, Parkwood. Tel: (011) 447 5804. Open Mon–Fri 0900–1700, Sat 1000–1700, Sun 1000–1500. Superb quality crafts, from black and white Mali mudcloths to finely etched Tuareg bowls. Not cheap, though.

Timbuktu Trading

Unit 1, Progress Park, 48 Richards Drive, Midrand. Tel: (011) 315 2363. Open Tue–Sat 0930–1630. You won't regret making the long drive from town – this showroom's crammed with lovely things (sheer Ethiopian *gabi* shawls; wooden doors made by Zimbabwe's Tonga tribe) from Africa's remotest corners.

Pretoria

The Lemon Lounge

Shop 10, Brooklyn Mall, Brooklyn. Tel: (012) 346 5082. Open Mon–Fri 0900–1800, Sat 0900–1500, Sun 1000–1300. New-Wave South African designer homeware, furniture, and 'lifestyle accessories' – look out for the divinely simple, paper-thin china bowls by local potter, Ant.

What to buy

The traditional *moraba-raba* board game, an African version of chess, makes a good souvenir. Two players manoeuvre counters (or 'cows') around holes in a wooden board until one has captured all his opponent's cows, and his 'king's kraal' is full.

Soweto

Soweto (short for SOuth WEstern TOwnships) is one of the great cities of South Africa. It has produced more Nobel Peace Prizewinners than anywhere else in the world, for example – yet it is a side to the country that few visitors (and indeed, few white South Africans) ever explore.

One reason, of course, is safety: black or white, it's not a good idea to visit as a lone wanderer. Try an organised tour, though, and you'll be collected from your Johannesburg hotel – probably late, true to African tradition – and catapulted straight down the **Golden Highway** in an air-conditioned minibus. Your first view of Soweto will come from a pedestrian bridge over the Old Potch Rd, one of only a handful of access routes (planning authorities limited entry points so the area could be speedily sealed off for security reasons).

Even on a bright summer's day, a pall of smoke hangs over the shacks and traditional 'matchbox' houses stretching away into the distance. Residents burn malodorous soft brown coal for cooking and heating, giving Soweto a distinctive smell and blocking out the sun on really bad days.

But your guide will not focus on the squalor, nor the smoking rubbish-tips which can be seen on most street corners. Most of the six million locals are proud of their city's political history, and everyone knows the humble matchbox house – now a museum – where the Mandela family lived until Madiba's release from prison in 1989. You'll also be shown **Freedom Square** in Dube suburb, commemorating the seminal student uprising of 16 June 1976.

After a glimpse of the poshest suburbs such as **Diepkloof Extension**, where fortress-like mansions belonging to the likes of Archbishop Desmond Tutu are crowded onto postage-stamp plots, you'll end up in one of Soweto's numerous *shebeens* (pubs), where you can get to grips with the city's feisty urban culture first-hand.

- **Jimmy's Face to Face Tours** (*tel: (011) 331 6109*) is the original township tour operator and still going strong.

- **Imbizo Tours** (*tel: (011) 838 2667*) offers night-time shebeen crawls and customised tours, plus the standard four-hour visit.

Mpumalanga

East of Gauteng, the Highveld comes to an abrupt halt at a mighty escarpment where wooded cliffs and waterfalls plunge 1000m to the Lowveld below. The subtropical savannah here is home to South Africa's best game parks, for it supports an extraordinary wealth of wildlife – from exotic birds and reptiles to the Big Five.

MPUMALANGA

BEST OF
Mpumalanga

Tourist information: **Graskop Tourist Information**: *Spar Centre, Pilgrim's Rd. Tel: (031) 767 1833. Open Mon–Fri 0830–1700, Sat 0900–1700, Sun 0900–1300.* **Lydenburg Tourist Information**: *Local Council Offices, Centraal St. Tel: (013) 235 2121. Open Mon–Fri 0730–1300, 1400–1630.* **Pilgrim's Rest Tourist Information**: *Main St, Upper Town. Tel: (013) 768 1060. Open daily 0900–1245, 1315–1630.* **Sabie Tourist Information**: *Main St. Tel: (013) 764 2281. Open Mon–Sat 0700–2000, Sun 0730–2000.*

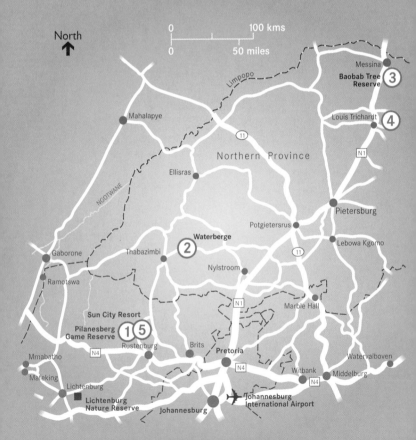

① The Mpumalanga Drakensberg

Just a few hours' drive from Gauteng, a network of spectacular roads skirts the steep eastern face of the Drakensberg range where it drops 1000m to the subtropical Lowveld below. This mountain region's one of South Africa's favourite holiday retreats, particularly as a stopover to or from the Kruger National Park. **Pages 132–133**

② Pilgrim's Rest

Once crowded with prospectors and fortune-seekers, this old gold rush village is now a major tourist attraction and a national monument. You can explore its beautifully restored corrugated-iron shops and monuments, or learn how to pan for gold at the Diggings Museum. **Page 133**

③ Blyde River Canyon

Eastern Mpumalanga is where you'll find one of the world's largest and loveliest gorges, crammed with mist forest, tumbling waterfalls and extraordinary rock formations. Take in all the best views on a half-day's drive, or try hiking and climbing in the nature reserve here. **Page 133 and opposite**

④ Kruger National Park

South Africa's flagship game reserve is as big as Wales, and has more mammal species than any other park in Africa. Thousands of animals and birds live here, including the Big Five – lion, elephant, buffalo, leopard and rhino. Undoubtedly one of the country's great wilderness experiences. **Pages 134–139**

⑤ Thulamela

In the far north of the Kruger National Park lie the ruined stone walls of a medieval royal village, where the ancestors of the modern-day Venda peoples once ruled a powerful city-state. Book for a guided tour of the site. **Pages 144–145**

Gorgeous gorge

A 29,000-hectare nature reserve encompasses some of the **Blyde River Canyon**'s most dramatic scenery, which you can explore on both short trails and overnight hikes. Best for short-stay visitors is the well-marked, five-hour **Belvedere Day Walk**, dropping down through thick forest along the eastern side of the canyon. Longer treks include the five-day 65km **Blyderivierspoort Hiking Trail**, taking in famous landmarks like Bourke's Luck Potholes and the Three Rondavels, with accommodation in overnight huts. For more information on both trails and accommodation within the **Blyderivierspoort Nature Reserve**, contact the **Mpumalanga Parks Board** (*tel: (031) 759 5300*).

The big game show

- The Kruger National Park's entrance gates close around 1830 during high season, so give yourself plenty of time to reach your rest camp on the day of arrival.
- Speed limits within the park are 50kmh on tarred roads and 40kmh on gravel roads.
- Try to avoid visiting during school holidays, when roads get pretty crowded and you could compete with a squash of 30 vehicles clustered round a lion kill.
- Malaria prophylactics are essential – consult your chemist before you travel.

The Mpumalanga Drakensberg

*Striking east from Johannesburg on the N4, it's 209km through sun-bleached wheat and cattle-ranching country to bleak little **Belfast**. A left turn here onto the R540 and a 93km drive north brings you to the farming centre of **Lydenburg** in the Drakensberg foothills – so far, so unremarkable, but the 45km trip east over the mountains to the timber-industry town of Sabie makes up for all that.*

Sabie

Originally built so supplies could be brought up from the coast to the Highveld goldfields, this steep road was much reviled by transport-riders as it made a particularly harrowing ox-wagon ride. During the Boer War, retreating Boers famously routed British forces here with two huge 150mm Creusot field guns nicknamed 'Long Toms', which they had laboriously dragged up the mountain slopes. Nowadays, the R37 coils serenely up, then down **Long Tom Pass**, with terrific views of undulating, forested hills.

Tranquil Sabie is encircled by soughing pine plantations, but a few patches of indigenous forest still cloak the mountain slopes nearby. They also glimmer with waterfalls; three of the prettiest – **Bridal Veil**, **Horseshoe** and finally **Lone Creek** – are well signposted just 7km west of town on the Old Lydenburg Rd. Most dramatic are the twin

Baker's designs

Sabie's pretty little St Peter's Church in Main St was designed in 1912 by the ubiquitous Sir Herbet Baker, the man behind Pretoria's Union Buildings and St George's Cathedral in Cape Town.

cascades of the **Mac Mac Falls** (14km to the north on the R532), that plummet 56m into a densely wooded gorge. They're named after the numerous Scottish diggers who worked claims here during the gold-rush years.

Pilgrim's Rest

North of Sabie, a 35km drive via the R532 and R533 leads to the photogenic Victorian gold-mining village of Pilgrim's Rest. After alluvial gold deposits ran out here in the 1970s, the entire town was declared a national monument and carefully restored to its red-roofed, turn-of-the-century quaintness. More tourist attraction than actual community, it's a nice place for a cup of tea and a stroll around – although the open-air **Diggings Site Museum** (*1km south of town on the Graskop Rd; daily tours 1000, 1100, 1200, 1400, 1500; £*) with its rough wattle-and-daub huts gives a glimpse of how tough the first miners really had it. Gold-panning demonstrations are held here, too.

Now retrace your route to little **Graskop** – splendidly situated right on the Escarpment's lip – and take the R534 heading north. After 6km, you'll reach the turn-off to **God's Window** viewpoint, a gap in the mountains with prodigious views over the Lowveld.

Blyde River Canyon

The best is yet to come, however; just visible to the north is Blyde River Canyon (*see also page 131*), at 26km long one of the world's largest and loveliest gorges. You can take in all the most gobsmacking views on a half-day's drive: following the curve of the R534 back onto the R532, and heading north, it's 28km to the turn-off for **Bourke's Luck Potholes** – fantastic rock formations sculpted by wind and river water – and a further 14km to the viewpoint over the round, weirdly symmetrical hills known as the **Three Rondavels**. From here, a spectacular 90km drive west onto the R36, down the **Abel Erasmus Pass**, brings you out at the canyon's base.

133

Kruger National Park: southern section

Kruger is the ultimate do-it-yourself wildlife-viewing experience. Good-value, self-drive safaris are the name of the game here, either camping at established campsites or using self-catering, thatched rondavels *(huts).*

Most roads are tarred, so there's no need for a 4WD vehicle, and almost all rest-camps have petrol stations, restaurants, shops and laundrettes. The southern reaches of the park have the widest range of landscapes and the greatest concentrations of game, but bear in mind this means the greatest concentrations of tourists, too.

The Kruger National Park: Tel: (013) 735 5611. Open daily 0530–1830 (but hours vary slightly every month). Admission: £. Book accommodation through the National Parks Board, PO Box 7400, Roggebaai, Cape Town 8012, tel: (021) 22 2810; or PO Box 787, Pretoria 0001, tel: (012) 343 1991.

Skukuza

Skukuza, the largest rest-camp and the park's administrative centre, is reached via **Paul Kruger Gate**, some 42km east of **Hazyview** on the R536. It's almost a village with two restaurants, a supermarket, post office, bank, car-hire agency, library and small airport – but the surrounding bushveld nevertheless offers some of the park's finest game-viewing. Rewarding drives include the road southeast along

the banks of the Sabie River to **Lower Sabie,** where you could spot hippos and crocs, along with lion, elephant, giraffe and perhaps even the rare nyala. Organised night drives offer a chance to see some of Kruger's more secretive creatures.

Pretoriuskop

28km from Hazyview.

Pretoriuskop, the third largest rest-camp and the park's oldest, is another easy drive from Hazyview, via **Numbi Gate**. Set in the park's most mountainous region – home to giraffe, kudu and a sizeable white rhino population – there's history here, too. Along the **Old Transport Rd** (Oude Wagenweg) running southeast, plaques mark the route followed in 1884 by the original bull terrier of *Jock of the Bushveld* fame and his transport-rider owner, Percy Fitzpatrick. Night drives are available.

Berg-en-Dal

11km from Malelane Gate.

The quickest route to Kruger from Johannesburg – a 410km drive on the N4 – deposits you at **Malelane Gate**, the park's southernmost. Berg-en-Dal is one of the newest rest-camps, set in hilly country overlooking the **Matjulu dam** where animals come to drink. You can look forward to a modern chalet here instead of the usual cylindrical hut, and there's a beautiful swimming pool, too. Organised bush drives are available.

Lower Sabie

35km north of Crocodile Bridge.

In an idyllic setting overlooking the Sabie River, Lower Sabie is justifiably one of Kruger's most popular camps. This is prime game-viewing territory – you could spot lion, cheetah, wild dog, kudu, giraffe, zebra, wildebeest and the ubiquitous impala. In the evening, many animals including elephant come to the river to drink.

Kruger National Park: central section

The wide, grassy plains sweeping through Kruger's central region make excellent grazing grounds for buffalo, zebra, wildebeest and impala, as well as the animals which prey on them – leopard, cheetah, wild dog and lion. In fact, according to park officials, this area has the largest population of lions in the world, so the odds on a sighting are definitely good.

If you've been exploring Blyde River Canyon, the quickest route to Kruger is via **Orpen Gate**, a 45km drive from **Klaserie** on the R531. **Orpen** rest-camp here is another entry-point camp with limited facilities; the main reason to stay is if you arrive too near gate-closing time to reach any of the larger, more distant camps. Luxuries are kept to a minimum in little **Tamboti** nearby, which has communal cooking and ablution facilities and accommodation in furnished tents. The substantial **Maroela** campsite 4km north is in a lovely position overlooking the Timbavati River.

Satara

48km from Orpen Gate.

Busy Satara is second only to Skukuza in size and has a rather clinical, impersonal atmosphere. The huts themselves, however, are all pleasantly shaded by mahogany and sausage trees, which are a magnet for birds – especially buffalo-weavers and starlings. A waterhole just outside the fence makes for great game-viewing in the early mornings and evenings. **Tshokwane** picnic site about 40km from camp on the road south to Skukuza is reputedly a hot spot for lions, and thus gets pretty chock-a-block with visitors, too.

Olifants

About 52km from Phalaborwa on the R71 via Phalaborwa Gate.

Thanks to its fabulous setting on a cliff overlooking the Olifants River, Olifants is one of Kruger's most sought-after camps. Game-spotting from the thatched main terrace, down over the fever-tree-fringed river, is almost always rewarding, as are drives through the surrounding bush (there's a boulder-covered hill about 12km down the road north to Letaba which is a famously good place to see the little klipspringer antelope). Make reservations early, though, as Olifants gets booked up fast in season.

Letaba

50km east from Phalaborwa Gate.

Letaba is spread along a bend in the beautiful river from which it takes its name, although for some reason very few huts were built with river views. Shaded by tall ilala palms and mopane trees, this is a great camp for elephant-spotting – especially from the restaurant's long veranda, with its views of the Letaba where the mighty mammals come to quench their thirst.

If that whets your appetite, the little **Prospectors' Museum** (*admission free*) here has all sorts of information on elephants, including a display on seven bulls legendary for their giant tusks (one weighing in at a whopping 71kg). Organised bush drives are also available.

Talamati, Balule, Shimuwini

Central Kruger's 'bushveld camps' include **Talamati** (*30km from Orpen Gate*), which has spartan facilities but a good setting in prime game-viewing country, and equally unsophisticated **Balule** (*11km south of Olifants*), where only an electric fence separates your hut from the bush. The chalets at **Shimuwini** (*50km north of Phalaborwa Gate*) overlook a dam shaded by giant sycamores, and are a big favourite with birdwatchers.

Tarred roads

Some visitors may have an aesthetic objection to driving through the wilderness on tarred roads, but park wardens would argue that these are actually environmentally friendly, preventing a build-up of choking dust.

137

Northern Kruger and the private reserves

The closer to the Zimbabwean border you travel in Kruger, the hotter and wilder it becomes. Not many visitors bother to explore this section, for its flat, mopane-dotted plains lack the concentration and variety of game found relatively easily down south.

Yet fans swear by the desolate beauty of the remote landscape and the game-spotting challenges it presents: this is where you'll see the larger antelope such as sable and tsessebe, marvellous birds (Cape parrot; tropical boubou), and it's also excellent country for elephant.

Mopani

74km from Phalaborwa Gate.

Mopani rest-camp is one of the park's newest. Its modern thatch-and-stone chalets are set on a rocky slope overlooking **Pioneer Dam**, which – as one of the north's few year-round water supplies – attracts a good variety of game, from elephant to hyena and antelope. Night drives are also available.

Shingwedzi

70km east of Punda Maria Gate, itself some 130km east of Louis Trichardt on the R524.

Shingwedzi is the largest of the three northern rest-camps. Set in spacious grounds liberally sprinkled with trees (palms and mopane) and lovely winter-flowering impala lilies, it also has a large swimming pool and a terraced restaurant overlooking the Shingwedzi River. The best game drive is south towards Letaba along the riverbank – **Kanniedood Dam**, 20km away, is a real gem. Night drives are available.

Punda Maria

10km east of Punda Maria Gate and 74km south of Pafuri Gate.

A two-and-a-half hour drive north from Shingwedzi brings you to Punda Maria rest-camp, just east of the Luvuvhu River.

Thanks to its thatched 1930s huts and pretty setting amidst groves of tall jackalberry and nyala trees, this little camp has a wonderfully romantic, time-warped feel, although it's seldom visited. Good excursions include the short drive south to **Dzundwini** hill (look out for Sharpe's grysbok here) and – heading north – the bridge over the **Luvuvhu**, an excellent birdwatching spot.

Bushcamps

Bushcamps include **Bateleur** (*37km southwest of Shingwedzi*) with a timber deck overlooking a seasonal waterhole, and the larger **Sirheni** (*28km northwest of Shingwedzi*), on the edge of **Sirheni Dam**.

The private reserves

In the 1960s and 1970s, various drought-stricken farms adjacent to the Kruger Park bought themselves a new lease of life by joining forces as private game farms and reserves. Most are unfenced, so wildlife from Kruger can move unimpeded across the region.

Hiking trails

Three-day wilderness hiking trails are conducted in the Kruger Park under the supervision of experienced, armed rangers. Ask for details when you book.

The three largest private reserves – **Sabi Sand**, **Manyeleti** and **Timbavati** – are home to numerous exclusive lodges and camps offering not just deluxe accommodation and fabulous cuisine, but off-road game drives in the company of experienced rangers. They show and explain the sub-plots (geology, butterflies, birds) as well as the star turns (the Big Five), and with two game drives per day, even a single night's stay can give a pretty good taste of Africa untamed.

Eating and drinking

*Trout has been farmed in the **Mpumalanga Drakensberg** since the 1950s, and it's a mainstay of restaurant menus in Escarpment towns, whether smoked and made into pâté, baked whole, or served up in a creamy soup. As the nearby **Lowveld** is big-game country, you'll also come across some unusual meats (wildebeest, impala and warthog, to name but a few), while locally-grown subtropical fruits and nuts are a staple of roadside stalls.*

Pubs and bars

The Royal Hotel

Main St, Upper Town, Pilgrim's Rest. Tel: (013) 768 1100. Open Mon–Thur 1000–2100, Fri–Sat 1000–2200. £. This charming Victorian hotel with its corrugated-iron façade is home to an equally delightful bar. The period furniture here originally belonged to a Catholic mission church in Mozambique – shipped out and painstakingly reinstalled in 1893.

Zeederburg Coach House

Ford St, Sabie. Tel: (013) 764 2630. Closed Sun pm and Tue. £. Set in a picturesque old Victorian house, this pleasant pub-cum-restaurant has a bohemian ambience that goes down well with a younger crowd.

Restaurants

Artists' Café
Hendriksdal, 15km south of Sabie on the R37. Tel: (013) 764 2309. Open daily lunch and dinner. ££. Hendriksdal's old railway station has been imaginatively converted to house this fine restaurant, with adjacent gallery (*see page 143*) and B&B facilities. Northern Italian menu; friendly service. Reservations essential.

Bag-dad Café
Sibelala Tourist Centre, 2km from White River on the R40 to Hazyview. Tel: (013) 751 1777. Open daily lunch and dinner. £. Tasty home cooking; they also do great picnic hampers with farm cheeses and breads.

De Kraal
Hazyview area. Tel: (013) 737 7853. ££. Attempts to recapture the 'field kitchen' atmosphere of the transport-rider days, with outdoor eating lit by paraffin lamps and a range of exotic meat dishes on the menu. Open for group bookings only, so phone ahead for reservations and directions.

Graskop Hotel
Cnr High St and Louis Trichardt Ave, Graskop. Tel: (013) 767 1244. ££. The restaurant here dishes up delicious meals with an emphasis on fresh local ingredients – but it opens only 'when there's a tour bus in', so phone ahead.

Harrie's
Louis Trichardt St, Graskop. Tel: (013) 767 1273. Open lunchtimes only. £. Legendary for its pancakes, both savoury and sweet.

Loggerhead Restaurant
Cnr Main and Old Lydenburg Rds, Sabie. Tel: (013) 764 3341. Closed Sun pm and Mon. £. Steakhouse with aspirations, offering competent cooking, an imaginative wine list and a few surprises – if you've ever wanted to try biltong salad, this is the place.

What to try

Staying in self-catering accommodation in the Kruger Park? Roadside vendors in the White River area sell exotic local produce (pecans, macadamia nuts, avocados, lychees and mangoes) worth stocking up on.

Theatre, performance and cinema

Botshabelo Historical Village

13km north of Middelburg on the N11. Tel: (013) 243 1319. Open Mon–Fri 0730–1630, Sat–Sun 1000–1600. Admission: £. The Middelburg region is the traditional home of the southern Ndebele, distinguished by a rich artistic tradition. This restored 19th-century mission station has some good examples of geometrically-patterned painted homes and intricately-beaded traditional costumes, and you can also watch Nedebele women at work painting murals, along with displays of traditional dancing and singing. Explore on your own or enquire at the open-air museum about guided tours.

Shopping

*If you're travelling to the Kruger Park's southern sector, it's worth considering making a brief detour to the little farming centre of **White River** on the R538. It's home to a growing number of artists, so there's interesting pickings here as far as arts and crafts are concerned.*

Artists' Café

Hendriksdal, 15km south of Sabie on the R37. Tel: (013) 751 2859. Open Mon–Fri 0800–1600, Sat 0900–1300. Showcases a mixture of work by local painters; call for an appointment and directions.

Bosch Studio

White River area. Tel: (013) 751 2859. Open Mon–Fri 0800–1600, Sat 0900–1300. The wares on offer at this little ceramics studio are definitely worth a look – but call first for an appointment and directions.

Eloff Studios

White River area. Tel: (013) 750 1884. Open Mon–Fri 0700–1700 and by appointment. Landscape and wildlife impressions, etchings and bronze sculptures. Call for directions.

White River Artists Trading Post

Christie's Village Mall, Theo Kleynhans St, White River. Tel: (013) 751 1053. Open Mon–Fri 0800–1600, Sat 0900–1300. A good cross-section of locally-produced crafts and artwork finds its way to this timber-framed outlet.

Rottcher Wineries

Nutcracker Valley, 2km south of White River on the R536. Tel: (013) 751 3886. Open Mon–Fri 0800–1700, Sat 0800–1500, Sun 1000–1500. Produces unusual wines made from oranges along with liqueurs; also houses the Wolhuters Gallery with local art displays.

What (not) to buy

You won't see ivory trinkets for sale in Kruger's curio shops: the park has suspended its controversial elephant culls and now relies on jumbo-sized doses of contraceptive vaccine to keep numbers down.

Born to be wild?

While the conventional view of the Kruger National Park is of an unspoilt wilderness, kept in pristine condition by a team of dedicated custodians, that's only half the story. Not only do the park's San rock art sites indicate that people had lived here for thousands of years, but the ruins of a major Iron Age settlement unearthed on a mountain near the Zimbabwean border reveal it as something of an archaeological treasure house.

Thulamela, as the site's known, was once a wealthy city-state that built sophisticated stone palaces, traded ivory as far afield as Africa's East Coast, and played an important role in sub-Saharan politics. It's thought that Thulamela's rulers were related to modern-day TshiVenda-speaking peoples, whose historical and cultural links with Zimbabwe are particularly strong.

MPUMALANGA

The story of the **Makuleke** is another, more recent instance of Kruger's complex past. Evicted from their ancestral grounds between the Levuvhu and Limpopo rivers in 1969 so that the park's fences could be extended to the Zimbabwean border, this clan was finally given back title to their land in 1998, as part of the new government's land reform programme. They have agreed not to reoccupy it on condition they benefit from new tourism developments within the park.

The Makuleke's eviction typifies the extraordinary zeal with which Kruger's apartheid-era administrators carried out their conservation mission. Right up until the end of the 1980s, the park's sensitive eastern border with Mozambique (a country sympathetic to the then-outlawed ANC) was patrolled by a quasi-military unit of rangers, trained by instructors from the SADF's 111 Battalion. Rangers still sometimes act as impromptu border-guards, intercepting illegal immigrants from Mozambique who have negotiated a terrifying pasage through the bush in order to seek back-door entry into South Africa.

These days, however, with the entire subject of heritage management up for debate in the new South Africa, the South African Parks Board does at least acknowledge that Kruger has a cultural history as well as splendid natural assets.

To book a guided tour of Thulamela, enquire at your rest-camp's reception desk.

The Far North

The creaking wheels of ox-wagons cut the first tracks of the Great North Rd, now the country's lifeline to Zimbabwe and the rest of Africa. The surrounding bushveld – hot, flat and thorny – is scattered with mountain ranges as remote as they are mysterious, home to the Python-God and the revered Rain Queen.

147

BEST OF
The Far North

*Tourist information: **North-West Province: Pilanesberg Information Centre**: Pilanesberg Game Reserve. Open Mon–Thur 0730–1630, Fri 0730–2000, Sat 0730–1630, Sun 0730–1530, closed daily 1300–1400. **The Waterberg: Nylstroom Tourist Information**: Public Library, Field St. Tel: (014) 717 5211. Open Mon–Fri 0900–1700, Sat 0900–1200. **Letaba: Tzaneen Tourism Information Centre**: 25 Danie Joubert St. Tel: (015) 307 1294. Open Mon–Fri 0800–1700, Sat 0800–1100. **The Far North and Venda: Soutpansberg Marketing Tourism & Information**: 54 Joao Albasini St, Louis Trichardt. Tel: (015) 516 0040. Open Mon–Sat 0800–1700, Sat 0800–1300.*

① Big Game vs the Big Smoke

It's easy to see why the Pilanesberg Game Reserve is North-West Province's biggest tourist draw. Set in the crater of a long-extinct volcano, it offers excellent game-viewing – including the Big Five – and comfortable accommodation only two hours' drive from Johannesburg. **Pages 150–151**

② Waterberg Riding Safaris

Horseback safaris are a feature of the unspoilt Waterberg massif. Riding through the cool montane grassland of the Conservancy Area, you could spot rhino, zebra and giraffe along with plenty of antelope and birds. Or grab a stetson and try your hand at cattle-mustering on a local dude ranch.
Page 153

③ Messina's Baobabs

These bulbous monster-trees – giants of the African bushveld – flourish in the hot, dry plains of the Far North, where the biggest are hollowed out and used as shops and even houses. Messina's Baobab Reserve protects a forest of fine specimens, some over 1000 years old. **Page 157**

④ Venda crafts

The Soutpansberg range is the traditional home of the vhaVenda people, known not only for their striking mystical beliefs but also their strong tradition of art and crafts – from woodcarvings and brightly-painted clay pots to decorated drums. **Pages 160–161**

⑤ Sun City

An over-the-top blend of tack, glitz and first-class service, South Africa's very own miniature Las Vegas makes a fun weekend break – particularly if you combine a stay with game-viewing in nearby Pilanesberg Game Reserve. **Pages 162–163**

Getting around

The Zion Christian Church, the largest independent black Christian grouping in the country, have their headquarters at **Zion City Moria** near Haenertsburg in the Letaba district, just off the R71. An amazing three million followers congregate here every Easter for a special annual celebration, leaving local roads extremely congested. Steer clear.

North-West Province

Wedged between the Free State and the Botswana border, much of this region is a chequerboard of wheat- and sunflower-fields, although the fact that its two main attractions – Sun City and the Magaliesberg Mountains – fall invitingly close to Gauteng means it scores well on the tourist front, too.

Rustenburg Nature Reserve

Tel: (014) 533 2050. Open daily 0700–1800. Admission: £.

The bustling little mining town of **Rustenburg** in the Magaliesberg foothills is just 104km west of Pretoria on the N4, and the obvious base for visiting the Rustenburg Nature Reserve 4km southwest (it's signposted from Wolmarans and Boekenhout Sts). This peaceful slice of mountain wilderness offers a great breather from city fumes, with hikes through aloe-speckled bushveld and well-wooded *kloofs* (gorges). The 2km **Vlei Ramble** has a viewing hut where you could spot a good variety of birds (including the rare black eagle and Cape vulture) and small antelope at close range. Longer hikes – with accommodation in basic huts – must be booked in advance.

Pilanesberg Game Reserve

Tel: (014) 555 6135. Open daily Apr–Aug 0530–1900, Sept–Mar 0500–2000. Admission: £.

About 45 minutes' drive north along the R565 is the glitzy gambler's paradise of **Sun City** (*see pages 162–163*) and the adjacent Pilanesberg Game Reserve, set round an extinct volcano crater with a lake at its core. This was Tswana cattle-grazing land until the 1970s, when it was controversially restocked with big game. The scenery (58,000 hectares of rolling Highveld bush, dotted with rocky outcrops) isn't as impressive as the big Lowveld reserves further north, but

it's certainly possible to see all the larger animals here, including lion, elephant, both black and white rhino and leopard, along with hundreds of different bird species.

The reception office at **Manyane Gate** and the park's information centre both have maps detailing the best game-viewing sites, including the cunning **Scavenger Hide** sitting just below ground level with angled, glassed-in viewing ports. Birdwatchers should head for the stilted hide on **Mankwe Dam**

Accommodation ranges from safari tents to self-catering chalets and luxurious **Tshukudu Lodge**, on a steep hill overlooking a wide, often game-filled plain.

Groot Marico

90km west of Rustenburg along the N4.

The sleepy one-street backwater of Groot Marico serves an isolated Afrikaner farming community which the writer **Herman Charles Bosman** turned into a legend. In the 1920s he spent six months working as a teacher here, an experience he encapsulated in a series of warm and witty short stories about the *backveld* way of life.

The Marico's other claim to fame is its celebrated *mampoer* (moonshine), distilled from an extraordinary range of sources including peaches and even chillies. Locals celebrate the lethal brew with an annual festival; if you'd like a sample, try the **Mampoer Route** (arranged on request; details from the tourist office) around local farm stills. The **Marico Oog**, a natural spring 20km south of town, makes a good swimming and picnic spot if you need somewhere to recover.

151

> " *The leopard stared at that rent in my trousers for quite a while, and my embarrassment grew. I felt I wanted to explain about the Government tax-collector and the barbed wire . . . I could not permit the wild animals of the neighbourhood to sneer at me.* "

Herman Charles Bosman, *In the Withaak's Shade,* **from** *Mafeking Road,* **1947**

Northern Province: the Waterberg

North of Gauteng, the veld fans out into hot yellow plains interrupted only briefly by a sprawl of low mountain ranges known collectively as the Waterberg.

Once the Big Five roamed this wild massif, although the white settlers who arrived in the 19th century soon shot out

the local game. Until the start of the 1990s it was a cattle-ranching area, but now many farms have been turned into conservation-orientated game and hunting reserves by their enterprising Afrikaner owners, and restocked with wildlife – from hippo and rhino to giraffe. The remote plateau has become a major ecotourism growth point.

Nylstroom

180km north of Pretoria on the N1, including a 10-km turn-off onto the R33.

The principal town in the district is the agricultural settlement of Nylstroom, so named because the first Voortrekker settlers to reach the area – having been on the road for years – decided the Mogalakwena River here must be the source of the Nile. There's not much to see, but take a look at the bust of **Eugène Marais** outside the public library in Field St. This great Afrikaner journalist, lawyer, natural historian, poet and author farmed in the Waterberg 1907–17, and it was here that he researched his best-known work, *The Soul of the Ape*. Plagued by ill health and increasingly addicted to morphine, he killed himself in 1936.

Waterberg Conservancy Area

Take the R33 west to Vaalwater, and then the (gravel) Melkrivier turn-off. The reserve's clearly signposted to the left, just before Melkrivier.

A significant chunk of the northeastern massif falls within the Waterberg Conservancy Area, three private reserves spread out along the banks of the Lapalala River. Best known is the 35,000-hectare **Lapalala Wilderness Area** (*130km northwest of Nylstroom; tel: (011) 453 7645; admission free, but accommodation ££–£££*) which made history in 1990 as the first game reserve to reintroduce the endangered black rhino to the area after a century's absence. You could also spot zebra, giraffe, kudu and the rare roan antelope here. Accommodation ranges from splendidly basic, electricity-free bush camps to self-catering chalets and the luxury **Rhino Tented Camp**, overlooking the river.

Activity-centred bush holidays – and particularly **riding trails** – are a feature of the Waterberg private reserves. For information on horse-riding safaris in the Lapalala Wilderness Area, contact **Equus Horse Safaris** (*tel: (011) 788 3923*). Other operators include **Horizon Horse Trails**, who offer cattle-mustering and cowboy campouts in the bush round sprawling **Triple B Ranch**, some 85km from Nylstroom (*tel: (0147552) and ask for 5404; cellphone: 083 287 2885*).

Marakele National Park

Book through the National Parks Board, PO Box 7400, Roggebaai, Cape Town 8012, tel: (021) 22 2810; or PO Box 787, Pretoria 0001, tel: (012) 343 1991.

Heading south along the R510, the iron-ore mining town of **Thabazimbi** lies on the outskirts of Marakele National Park, one of South Africa's newest. With 60,000 hectares of craggy, stream-cooled Waterberg scenery, plus an impressive supply of relocated animals (including elephant), it's sure to be a big draw. At the moment, though, facilities are still pretty limited, and you can only visit with a 4WD.

153

Northern Province: Letaba

Another significant set of mountains – this time, the mighty Drakensberg – starts to rise up from the thorny bushveld just east of the provincial capital, Pietersburg (130km north of Nylstroom on the N1). At the base of these foothills is the fertile Letaba region.

It's largely tea-producing country but also liberally scattered with lakes, lush stands of indigenous forest and enchanting waterfalls – so a big hit with walkers and anglers, which is why country lodges and upmarket guesthouses are in such plentiful supply.

The Magoebaskloof and Tzaneen

Beyond the old gold-rush village of **Haenertsburg** (*60km east of Pieterbsurg*) the R71 follows a beautiful route to Tzaneen via the misty slopes of the high Magoebaskloof. It's a drive to savour, the road twisting through pine plantations and dimly-lit, creeper-shrouded forest, with dazzling glimpses of distant countryside and rolling tea-estates. Some 11km beyond the Magoebaskloof Hotel, a 3.5km side road leads left into **Woodbush State Forest** (*clearly signposted*) and the track for Debengeni Falls, one of the most scenic swims in South Africa – in a deep, pot-shaped scoop of rock, the final plunge-pool in a lovely line of waterfalls.

> " *There . . . lay the hideous little monkey frame, covered with crinkled yellow parchment, that had once been the glorious She. Alas! It was no hideous dream – it was an awful and unparalleled fact!* "
>
> **Rider Haggard, *She*, 1887**

Back on the R71, the road continues through banana groves and emerald tea-fields to **Tzaneen** (*104km east of Pietersburg*), the Letaba's low-key commercial centre. Sights are few, apart from the tiny **Tzaneen Museum** (*Public Library, Agatha St;*

open Mon–Fri 0900–1700, Sat 0900–1300; admission: £), well worth visiting if you'd like some light shed on local legends such as the extraordinary Rain Queen (*see below*).

Most popular of the walks webbing the Tolkienesque goblin-forest of Magoebaskloof is the 3km **Lesodi Trail**, an easy stroll that starts out from the Magoebaskloof Hotel on the R71. Longer treks include the two-day **Debengeni Trail**, with overnight accommodation in basic cabins – or try the three-day Dokolewa Trail through nearby De Hoek Forest (*signposted off the R71 about 22km west of Tzaneen*). Booking is essential on these longer hikes; details from the tourist office.

Modjadji and the Rain Queen

Some 35km north of Tzaneen lies unassuming little **Modjadji**, the mountain homestead of the revered **Rain Queen**. Since the 16th century a dynasty of female rulers – all named Modjadji – has ruled the local Lobedu clan, who believe the queen has the power to make rain. The Victorian novelist Rider Haggard used her as the inspiration for his overwrought epic, *She*.

On a hilltop close to the royal family *kraal* is a forest of rare and ancient **cycads**, which the Lobedu regard as sacred to the Rain Queen. It's the highlight of the 300-hectare **Modjadji Nature Reserve** (*tel: (015) 23252 and ask for 5; open daily 0900–1600; admission: £*), which also offers huge views down over the Lowveld and some rewarding short trails through the subtropical bush. Tourist amenities leave something to be desired – unflushable flush-loos and a lack of running water – although there is a well-stocked souvenir

shop. *Take the R71 east out of Tzaneen towards Gravelotte, turn left onto the Deer Park road and follow the signs.*

The Far North and Venda

Oxen pulling Voortrekker wagons first trod the Great North Rd, now the main motorway linking Pretoria with Zimbabwe's Beit Bridge. **Louis Trichardt** *(* 112km north of Pietersburg*), the Far North's main settlement, is named after one of the pioneers' doughtiest leaders – although shrouded as it is in an atmosphere of permanent midday torpor, this joint isn't exactly jumping.*

A pleasant alternative is the little **Ben Lavin Nature Reserve** (*some 9km southeast of town on the R578; tel: (015) 516 4534; open daily 0600–1800; admission: £*) which has a decent rest-camp and some good short bushveld walks where you might spot zebra and giraffe.

Soutpansberg mountains

Looming over Louis Trichardt is the impressive Soutpansberg range, the most northerly in South Africa. Its lush southern foothills are swathed in exotic plantations from avocado to banana, but these uplands still offer a few pockets of ancient forest, complete with giant yellowwoods. **Hangklip Forest Reserve** (*3km northeast of Louis Trichardt on the N1; admission: £*) has some particularly scenic picnic spots.

Thohoyandou

Heading east in the shadow of the mountains along the R524, it's a 70km drive from Louis Trichardt to scraggy modern Thohoyandou, capital of the Venda region. This remote corner of the northeastern Soutpansberg became an 'official homeland' under apartheid, but for all that the vhaVenda's people's ancient culture – steeped in myth and magic – has remained more or less intact.

The baobab

The baobab can live for many hundreds of years, but when one dies, the end is dramatic. In a few months, the fibrous wood disintegrates and simply collapses in on itself, disappearing so suddenly that it was once thought baobabs ignited spontaneously and burned away.

In the cool, dimly-lit depths of the dense indigenous forests northwest of town are gravel tracks leading to mysterious **Lake Fundudzi**, lair of the great Python God of fertility, placated annually with gifts of beer poured onto the water. No maps are available, for this is a holy site, which may be visited only with permission from the local authority.

You can view the lake from a respectful distance, however: head north out of Thohoyandou, turn left onto the R523 and follow it west via **Sibasa**, climbing up the fertile plateau with its clusters of traditional villages. At the summit of the (signposted) **Thate Vondo Pass**, turn right onto a gravel road leading to **Thate Vondo Forest**. Bear straight ahead from the entrance gate for some 10km, then turn right and after 700m, right again at the fork. Keep going straight for 4km, take the next road leading right and then turn almost immediately right again, following the fence. Fundudzi glimmers tantalisingly below.

Messina

After the wooded valleys of the Soutpansberg, the 60km drive north to the old copper-mining town of Messina seems especially hot and taxing. Lending dramatic character to the monotonous bushveld are scattered armies of **baobab** trees, bulbous giants which – according to legend – the gods planted upside down as a joke. Indeed, Messina's most interesting feature is its encircling **Baobab Nature Reserve** (*entrance 6km south of town, and clearly signposted; admission: £*) containing 1000 or more splendid specimens. Many are over 1000 years old; all are national monuments.

From Messina, it's just 16km to the border and the 'great, grey-green, greasy Limpopo', as Kipling described it.

Eating and drinking

All sorts of exotica find their way onto rural Highveld restaurant menus. In the Far North, baobab and marula fruit are ubiquitous in season – the latter at its tastiest when made into jelly and served with venison.

By contrast, the cool and misty mountain ranges yield subtropical delicacies such as lychees, avocados and pecan nuts, while trout grow fat in local dams. Heady peach-flavoured *mampoer* (moonshine) from the Marico district and marula liqueur are two popular tipples to watch out for.

Pubs and bars

Letaba: Sunlands Farm & Nursery Baobab Bar

28km north of Tzaneen near Modjadji Nature Reserve (the tourist office can provide maps and directions). Tel: (015) 309 9039. £. This farm's showpiece is a monster baobab with a pub inside. It's only open on request, though, so phone ahead.

The Marico District: Bosveld Hotel

Paul Kruger St, Groot Marico. Tel: (014) 503 0045. Closed Sun. £. Houses a lively Afrikaner bar where on a good night, you could spot some of the more convivial locals kicking up their heels to a blast of traditional *sakkie-sakkie* music.

The Soutpansberg: Bergwater Hotel

5 Rissik St, Louis Trichardt. Tel: (015) 516 0262. Closed Sun. £. Quiet, unassuming bar with hospitable service.

The Waterberg: Vaalwater Hotel

Voortrekker Rd, Vaalwater. Tel: (014) 755 3686. Closed Sun. £. The bar here's very popular with Afrikaner farmers and big-game hunters passing through on safari. Not really the sort of place, then – if you're a bloke – to order a Babycham.

Restaurants

Letaba

Coach House Hotel

Old Coach Rd, Tzaneen. Tel: (015) 307 3641. Open daily lunch and dinner. ££. Classy little country house hotel – antique-filled, with plenty of roaring fires and great views – which has won many awards, not least for its cooking.

Glenshiel Country Lodge

Haenertsburg area. Tel: (015) 276 4335. Open daily lunch and dinner. ££. One of the top country lodges in South Africa. Deft, imaginative menu, with good use of local ingredients such as wild mushrooms and fresh trout.

Magaliesberg: Karl's Bauernstube

Rustenburg. Tel: (014) 537 2128. Closed Sat lunch, Sun dinner, all day Mon. £. This good-value outfit dishing up German food and beer is about as good as it gets in the Rustenburg area.

Soutpansberg: Ingwe Ranch Motel

Louis Trichardt area. Tel: (015) 517 7078. Open daily lunch and dinner. £. Surprisingly tasty fare, despite an undue emphasis on meat.

Theatre, performance and cinema

Letaba

Tsonga Kraal Open-air Museum

Hans Merensky Nature Reserve, Tzaneen area. Tel: (015) 386 8727. Guided tours Mon–Fri. At this rural village just north of Letsitele on the R529 there are regular performances of traditional singing and dancing; you can also watch Tsonga iron-forgers and potters at work.

The Magaliesberg

Music in the Mountains

Tel: (014) 577 1350. Summer (Dec–Jan) is the season for weekend classical concerts in the well-manicured grounds of the Mount Grace, an upmarket country house hotel in the lush Magaliesberg foothills. It's an hour's drive from Johannesburg; take the R24 heading west to Magaliesburg town, and follow the signs. Call for programme details.

159

Shopping

Letaba: Pekoe View Tea Garden & Shop

Sapekoe Tea Estates, Tzaneen. Tel: (015) 307 3120. Open daily 1000–1700. Signposted off the R71, near the R36 junction. You can buy packets of locally-grown tea here, but the best reason to visit is for the splendid views. Well-placed tea garden, too.

The Magaliesberg

Margaret Roberts Herbal Centre

Brits area. Tel: (012) 504 1729. Open Wed only 0830–1600. Take the R513 from Pretoria towards Hartbeespoort Dam, turn left onto Rd 16, and follow the signs. Stand at the door and breathe deeply. This spacious apothecary-style shop stocks all sorts of aromatherapeutic and culinary herbs, as well as plant-guru Roberts' own-label range.

Wegraakbos Dairy

Haenertsburg area. Tel: (015) 276 1811. Open Mon–Fri 0700–1700, Sat–Sun 0700–1130; tours daily at 0930 (£). Take the R528 heading southeast out of Haenertsburg and after 4km take the (gravel) turn-off for the Cheerio Gardens. The turn-off to the dairy is clearly signposted some 2km further on. Great little old-fashioned dairy where cheese is made in a vast copper pot over a roaring fire.

Venda: Tsonga Textiles

Off the R578 between Elim and Giyani Tel: (015) 556 3214. Open Mon–Fri 0800–1630. This rural workshop produces bright, screen-printed clothes and tablecloths in traditional designs, but also stocks a good selection of Venda crafts – from wooden carvings to clay pots. Head east along the R578 and pass through Elim; the (gravel) turn-off is poorly signposted on the left, some 5km further on.

What to buy

Venda has produced many well-known artists; Shangaan wood-carver Jackson Hlungwane and sculptress Noria Mabasa are particularly highly rated.

Tip

Bear in mind as you explore the rural dorps of the northern regions that this is traditionally the last refuge of conservative whites, many of whom have not adjusted well to the end of apartheid.

161

PROFILE

Sun City

*South Africa's answer to Las Vegas lies just 90 minutes' drive west of Johannesburg off the N4. This famous resort houses casinos, hotels, restaurants, cinemas, a huge auditorium and two world-class, Gary Player-designed golf courses, one of which has a water hazard inhabited by live crocodiles. Most over-the-top of all is the **Lost City Complex**, in which an enormous African 'palace' (or rather, a lavish five-star hotel) rises from an imported tropical jungle setting, complete with artificial beach and wave pool. Special effects such as the juddering '**Bridge of Time**' – wreathed in clouds of hypoallergenic smoke – complete the fantasy.*

The brains behind it all? Step forward, **Sol Kerzner**, the flamboyant Russian-immigrant boxer-turned-businessman

whose company Sun International now operates hotels and gaming resorts around the world. Kerzner's shrewdest move was to mastermind the erection of casino resorts in the poverty-stricken 'tribal homelands', which under apartheid were supposedly separate countries (Sun City itself was established in the former homeland of Bophutatswana). The country's white Calvinist rulers might have forbidden gambling, topless showgirls and – heaven forbid – sex across the colour bar, but no such strictures applied in these so-called independent states. White South Africans flocked across the borders in large numbers, and Kerzner's fortunes were assured.

Now that gambling's been legalised, numbers have thinned out a bit – yet Sun City's unique blend of tack, glitz and (as far as the sumptuous Palace Hotel goes, anyway) top-class service remains undiminished. It's undoubtedly a fun weekend break, especially if you combine a stay with game-viewing in the adjacent **Pilanesberg Game Park**.

To reach Sun City from Johannesburg, take the R24 for Rustenburg until the junction with the N4, and then take the first right turn onto the R565 and follow the signs. There's a small admission fee. If you arrive by plane (the airport's 7km away), a free monorail runs from the entrance to the **Welcome Centre** (*tel: (01465) 71544; open Sun–Thur 0900–2200, Fri–Sat 0900–0200*), which can also advise on the range of accommodation available.

Lifestyles

Shopping, eating, children and nightlife in South Africa

LIFESTYLES

Shopping

Shopping malls

International mall culture is alive and well in South Africa's major cities. Locals love these one-stop suburban shopping complexes with their hundreds of outlets – including hotels, restaurants, bars, banks, cinemas and supermarkets – and use them as places to socialise as well as shop. Johannesburg's glossiest example is **Sandton Square** in the northern suburb of Sandton; in Cape Town, mall rats head for **Cavendish Square** in Claremont. Durban's showpiece mall is a converted city-centre railway workshop called, rather unimaginatively, **The Workshop**. All include upmarket craft and curio outlets of varying quality (see the city chapters for more details).

Street markets

In the bigger towns you'll be hard-pressed to avoid what's grandly known as 'the informal sector' –

from inferior-quality soapstone curios and stolen car parts to fine carvings and crafts. Best buys here are salad bowls and servers made from mopane or tambotie wood, wire sculptures (*see page 169*) and baskets. Haggling is expected.

Craft markets

We have listed the best places to buy crafts in the relevant shopping sections within the guide, but these markets deserve a special mention:

Cape Town: Greenmarket Square Market *Greenmarket Square, City Centre. Open Mon–Sat and public holidays 0900–1700.* Long-running 'flea' offering a good selection of arts and crafts, curios and clothing in a beautiful oak-shaded cobbled square.

Gauteng: Irene Village Market *Smuts House Museum, Nelmapius Rd, Irene, Pretoria. Tel: (012) 667 1176. Second and last Sat of the month 0900–1400.* Outstanding craft market held in a field outside Pretoria. Ring for directions.

Durban: The Point Waterfront Flea Market *The Point, Point Rd. Open Sat–Sun and public holidays 0830–1600.* Outdoor stalls offering a huge variety of

pavement hawkers, in other words – energetically flogging everything

food and goods, including ceramics, jewellery, textiles and leather goods.

VAT refunds

VAT of 14 per cent is levied on most goods, as well as hotel accommodation, transport and tours. In shops, the price you see marked on the item includes the tax. Non-resident foreign visitors qualify for a VAT refund at points of international departure, providing the value of each invoice for the goods purchased exceeds R50, and the total value of all items purchased exceeds R250. You'll need to present the goods themselves along with the original invoice, your passport and a VAT refund control sheet (available from the retailer).

Business hours

Most shops and supermarkets open Mon–Fri 0800–1630, Sat 0830–1230, although in the main centres opening hours are likely to be longer. Many shopping malls also open on Sun

mornings. In smaller towns and rural areas, businesses often shut for lunch between 1300 and 1400.

Best local products

Gold and diamonds

Johannesburg – 'spinning on a hub of gold', as Negley Farson described it – is the best place to buy gold and diamonds. You can visit a concentration of jewellery manufacturers, diamond cutters and associated industries at the **SA Diamond Centre** (*240 Commissioner St; tel: (011) 334 8897*), which has gold as well as quality diamonds for sale. Their hour-long tour is worth doing if you're seriously planning to buy, and includes a presentation on the cutting and polishing process as well as the history of the South African diamond industry. They will pack and ship items anywhere.

Cape wine

A reliable service is provided by **Steven Rom** (*Galleria Centre, 76 Regent Rd, Sea Point; tel: (021) 439 6043*), who will deliver gift packs of selected South African wines around the globe (six bottles minimum). If you're not planning to visit the Winelands, Johannesburg's **Benny Goldberg's** (*Louis Botha Ave, Kew; tel: (011) 786 3670*) has a huge selection of local wines – indeed, it claims to be the country's largest off-licence. Duty-free shops at South Africa's international airports stock a reasonable selection, too.

Vintages to look out for include **Klein Constantia**'s 1992 Noble Late Harvest Sauvignon Blanc, along with Stellenbosch-based Plaisir de Merle's 1993 Merlot. **Buitenverwachting**'s 1991 Christina Bordeaux Blend is seriously good stuff, as is the 1994 **Thelema** Cabernet Sauvignon, again from Stellenbosch. For a truly indigenous flavour, you can't go wrong with the 1989 **Kanonkop** Auction Reserve Pinotage, a full and complex red wine made from South Africa's own noble grape.

Traditional beadwork

Brightly-coloured ethnic beadwork in geometric patterns is one of South Africa's most distinctive crafts. Traditionally, pieces were produced to mark social status along with rituals such as puberty, marriage and motherhood, and were often colour-coded. The magnificent beaded jewellery produced by the **Ndebele**, who live on the Highveld, is much prized by collectors, as are the filigree-like chains of authentic **Zulu** beadwork from KwaZulu-Natal.

African pots

Authentic **Zulu** pots are not thrown on a wheel but fashioned from fat coils of clay, which are then smoothed and fired. Their traditional shiny black coating comes from a mixture of animal fat, powdered manure and gooseberry leaves, painstakingly applied. Thanks to the easy availability of commercial crockery, the real thing is getting more and more difficult to find – you'll find this

reflected in the price. Ornamental pots from **Venda** in Northern Province, meanwhile, are more widely available, and with their geometric patterns and bright colours make particularly nice souvenirs.

Coathanger wire sculptures

Intricate wire windmills with whirring vanes are one of the Eastern Cape's most endearing local crafts – they're sold from the side of the road in rural areas, as well as in craft shops. Johannesburg's township crafters are also enthusiastic about coathanger wire as a medium, and you'll find street markets in the Rosebank area packed with amazingly inventive pieces from miniature saxophones to bicycles, along with fruit bowls, bathroom accessories and Christmas-tree decorations.

Export restrictions

International trade in sea turtle products and wild cat skins (ie leopard) is illegal, while restrictions have been placed on reptile skins, wild birds, tortoiseshell and coral along with certain seashells and plants. Check that you aren't buying a threatened species before you hand over your money. The CITES ban on trading in ivory has now been lifted, so choosing whether to buy or not is down to your conscience alone.

Eating out

While South Africa's diverse ethnic groupings all have their own styles of cooking, there is not really any such thing – yet – as a unified 'South African cuisine'. Few restaurants feature dishes from the whole spectrum of Rainbow Nation food (although these have been on the increase since the end of apartheid), and indeed there are only a few culinary traditions, like the braaivleis *(barbecue), which are enjoyed at home right across the board. Nonetheless, visitors can look forward to a wide range of styles and flavours, from fresh seafood and Cape Malay curries to hearty, meaty Afrikaner cuisine.*

Restaurants

Thanks to the weak rand, restaurants offer terrific value compared with the UK or the USA. Most establishments are licensed, unless they're Cape Malay (*see opposite*). Most also close on Monday evenings, in which case a hotel dining room is probably your best bet.

You'll find some of the country's finest restaurants in the **Winelands** region of the Western Cape, although all the main centres have their share of good eateries. American-style **steakhouse chains** such as Steers and the Spur are still the first choice for most families wanting a meal out, though. Check out the latest additions to the South Africa's culinary map by accessing the reliable *Nederburg/ Style Restaurant Guide* on the web: *www.webfeat.co.za/style.*

Cape seafood

The icy Atlantic washing the Cape's West Coast spawns some fabulous seafood – notably *perlemoen* (abalone), **crayfish** (rock lobster), **squid**, **oysters** and **mussels**. The best place to sample it is at one of the West Coast's celebrated **open-air restaurants** – no-frills affairs set right on the beach, where the food's cooked before your eyes over an open fire. Go for a swim between courses!

Cape Malay cooking

Soon after the Dutch first settled at the Cape in the 17th century, boatloads of slaves were shipped out from Holland's East Indies territories to serve the new settlement. Slowly but surely, cooks transformed their masters' stolid recipes with the subtly spiced and seasoned flavours of Java, Ceylon and Malaya, creating dishes which are now a cornerstone of Cape cuisine.

Specialities include *smoorsnoek* (braised snoek – a firm-fleshed, barracuda-like fish), *breyani* (rice pilau) and *bobotie* (a spicy minced-lamb stew topped with a savoury egg custard). In spring, look out for *waterblommetjie bredie*, lamb ragout flavoured with peppery water-hawthorn buds – a kind of pondweed. In true Eastern tradition, all these dishes are served with turmeric-flavoured rice, sambals and bowls of coconut. In true Muslim tradition, few Cape Malay restaurants serve alcohol – check when you book.

Black 'soul food'

For most black working-class city dwellers, a slap-up Sunday lunch is fried beef chops, a mound of yellow cornmeal and a fiery salad called

chakalaka made from raw tomatoes, onion, chilli and sweet peppers. You'll find this on the menu at township *shebeens* (pubs), too, along with fried chicken, *samp* (maize hominy grits) and *ting* (sour porridge).

A favourite rural dish is *morogo* – leaves from a kind of saltbush cooked spinach-style, and eaten with *phutu pap* (cornmeal porridge) and meat gravy. **Mopani worms** are another traditional source of protein; today you're likely to find them on the menu in upmarket urban African restaurants, served with chilli sauce.

Boerekos

Quite literally, farmer's food –
hearty, rib-sticking stuff which has
its cholesterol-clogged roots in 17th-
century Dutch country cooking. It's
strong on offal, from calf's head
brawn to tongue with raisin sauce,
and rich puddings are a speciality,
too – look out for **Cape Brandy
Pudding**, an alcohol-soused date-
and-nut concoction, served with
thick cream. Quality preserves are
another strong point: *boeremeisies*
('farmer's girls'), apricots preserved
in Cape brandy, are a good buy at
farm stalls.

fruity 'New World' styles so popular
abroad. While the overall standard
is still patchy, you can look forward
to a handful of gems (*see page 167*),
and they're extremely good value for
money. If you're visiting the Cape,
the best place to start is by touring
the **wine estates** themselves
(*see pages 54–55*).

South Africans are great **beer**
drinkers, and consume vast amounts
of locally-brewed lagers such as
Castle and Lion, always served
chilled. Imported beers are starting
to become more widely available.

Wine, beer and spirits

South Africa's wine industry
underwent something of a revolution
in the 1990s. Shaking off a centuries-
old attachment to French- and
German-style wine production, Cape
wine-makers have been at pains to
learn new skills and create the ripe,

Another strong contender for the
national drink is **brandy**, usually
drunk *dop en dam* (with a dash
of water) or with cola. **Moonshine**
– known here as *witblits* and
mampoer – still plays an important
part in Afrikaner folklore; annual
festivals are held in the Groot
Marico region on the Highveld to
celebrate the lethal brew.

Informal eating

Biltong: Strips of salted, air-dried venison kept the 19th-century Boers going on their long treks through the interior, and *biltong* (made from every kind of meat, including ostrich) remains a favourite South African snack even today.

Braaivleis: Every weekend, in gardens and national park picnic sites across the land, the air turns blue with barbecue smoke as one of the most deep-rooted South African rituals – the family *braaivleis* – gets underway. The traditional combination is vast quantities of **lamb chops** and *sosaties* (kebabs), a coriander-flavoured sausage known as *boerewors*, and salads, baked potatoes and *mielies* (corn-on-the-cob) on the side.

Bunny chow: A traditional Durban take-away, this is a hollowed-out loaf of bread filled with steaming meat or bean curry.

Koeksisters: Most bakeries sell these syrup-coated plaits of fried dough, traditionally served with coffee at the end of a meal.

Peri-peri sauce: A hot chilli-based seasoning which found its way onto South African menus courtesy of the Portuguese community. It's most often served with grilled chicken or prawns.

Roosterkoek: Visit any Afrikaner fête or market and you'll see someone cooking these square griddle-cakes on open fires. They're at their best fresh and hot, split open and filled with butter and jam.

Rusks: Hard, dried sweet bread rolls – *beskuit* in Afrikaans – were another Trekboer staple. Today, they're the standard accompaniment to early-morning coffee.

173

South Africa with children

Thanks to the sunny weather, South Africans put a good deal of emphasis on the outdoor life – which means lots of al fresco *pursuits for visiting children to enjoy. Otherwise, the homegrown 'kid's culture' is pretty Americanised, with US fashions, food, pop stars and TV programmes leading the way. In cities, look out for the Steer and Spur steakhouse chains which are both well geared up for children, offering kid's menus and helpful staff.*

The short, self-guided trails cutting through the Garden Route's **Tsitsikamma National Park** are especially good for children. Following the coloured arrows, they'll see vervet monkeys along with plenty of birds and clearly-labelled exotic trees. There's safe swimming in the rockpools linking the park's sandy bays, while dolphins are often spotted in the waves beyond – and sometimes Cape clawless otters, too. *Open daily 0530–2130. Admission: £. Book accommodation through the National Parks Board, PO Box 7400, Roggebaai, Cape Town 8012, tel: (021) 22 2810; or PO Box 787, Pretoria 0001, tel: (012) 343 1991.*

Children over 12 can explore the **Kruger National Park** on guided wilderness trails led by armed rangers, encountering all sorts of birds and mammals at close range. Sleeping in rustic huts, they'll also learn basic bushcraft and survival techniques, and enjoy campfire cookouts at night. *Tel: (013) 735 5611. Open daily 0530–1830 (but hours vary slightly every month). Admission: £. Book trails through the National Parks Board, PO Box 7400, Roggebaai, Cape Town 8012, tel: (021) 22 2810; or PO Box 787, Pretoria 0001, tel: (012) 343 1991.*

At Durban's **Waterworld** (*Battery Beach Rd; tel: (031) 332 9776; admission: £*) opposite Country Club Beach, kids can have fun on the lazy River Ride, eight different water-slides, the Water Playground and lots more. Entrance fee covers full use of the park for the day. For safe sea bathing, **Anstey's** and **Brighton Beaches** are uncrowded and sandy. Or try rocky **Treasure Beach**, which has a pristine stretch of tidal pools at its southern end.

The **Outeniqua Choo-Tjoe** is a veteran steam train with timber-and-leather fitted carriages which plies a picturesque 68km route from **George** on the Garden Route to **Knysna**. One-way trips – through dark tunnels and over high bridges, past beaches, lakes and forest – take two and a half hours, and can be linked to a return shuttle service. *George Station, Market St. Tel: (044) 801 8288. Departures Mon–Sat 0930, 1300. Tickets: £; under-3s travel free; concessions available for under-16s.*

Cape Town's **South African Museum** is the oldest and best natural history museum in the country. Biggest hits with kids are the ancient reptiles, the lifelike diorama of a San bushcamp and the evocative Whale Well, alive with eerie underwater sounds. *25 Queen Victoria St. Open daily 1000–1700. Admission: £, free Wed.*

The open-air **Kimberley Mine Museum** is an imaginative reconstruction of the original diamond-rush town, spread along the Big Hole's western edge. Kids can haul up a bucket of gravel and sift through it at a sorting table, looking for diamonds, take a ride on a Victorian tram, and try their luck in the old skittle alley. *Tucker St. Open daily 0800–1800. Admission: £.*

After dark

Clubs and discos

Cape Town: night owls head for the area around **Long, Lower Loop** and **Bree Streets** in the city centre, abuzz with clubs, pubs and restaurants. The **V&A Waterfront** at the harbour's edge is a good bet for restaurants and cafés – some venues offer live jazz, too.

Durban: upmarket Morningside suburb's **Florida Rd** pulls crowds of 20- and 30-somethings to its bistros, bars and clubs.

Johannesburg: by day it's crammed with shoppers and ladies-who-lunch,

but the glossy northern suburb of **Rosebank** heats up considerably after dark as drinkers and clubbers pack out the dance and music venues.

Listings

Check local daily newspapers for entertainment listings. The weekly *Mail & Guardian* newspaper (published Fri), and the monthly magazine *SA City Life (www.sacitylife.com)* both have very good coverage on major cities.

Music festivals

Rustler's Valley Easter Festival

Rustler's Valley, Ficksburg. Tel: (051) 933 3939. Early Apr. This beautiful corner of the Eastern Free State hosts South Africa's very own version of Glastonbury – four days of music (local and international DJs and live bands), plus craft markets and plenty of New Age therapies to get you in the mood.

Splashy Fen

Splashy Fen Farm, Underberg, southern Drakensberg. Tel: (031) 23 9812. Website: www.splashyfen.co.za. Early May. A trout farm in the scenic Drakensberg foothills is the suitably mellow venue for this laid-back folk festival, showcasing both international and South African acoustic and folk musicians.

Oppikoppi

Thabazimbi. Tel: (014) 786 0597. Website: www.oppikoppi.co.za. Mid Aug. For a few days each year, a lonely bushveld campsite in the Waterberg is transformed into a heaving mass of liggers, hippies, punks and wannabes as the most popular event on the South African music calendar gets underway. Features live jazz, reggae, rock and homegrown African and Afrikaner sounds.

Theatre, classical music and opera

Under apartheid, the classical performing arts were nurtured by four provincial performing arts councils which were subsidised by the government. Now these bodies (deemed 'Eurocentric' by the ANC) have had their subsidies transferred to a new National Arts Council, which funds artists and promotes the Africanisation of the arts instead. The classical performing arts companies have had to look to private enterprise to top up their radically slashed subsidies. As a result, the financial future of the country's various ballet schools, opera companies and orchestras remains in a somewhat precarious state.

Cape Town:

The Baxter Theatre Centre

Main Rd, Rosebank. Tel: (021) 685 7880. A showcase for innovative contemporary material as well as classics.

The Nico Theatre Centre

DF Malan St, Foreshore. Tel: (021) 21 5470. The city's most prestigious performance venue, with an opera house and two theatres.

Durban:

Bartle Arts Trust (BAT) Centre

45 Maritime Place, Small Craft Harbour, Esplanade. Tel: (031) 332 0451. Innovative community arts complex with dance and drama studios plus craft galleries and shops. The BAT Deck venue here hosts free sundowner jazz concerts every Friday. *Open Tue–Fri 0830–1630, Sat–Sun 0900–1700.*

Durban Playhouse Theatre Complex

Cnr St Thomas and Smith Sts, City Centre. Tel: (031) 369 9555. Call for programme details. An opera house and five theatres, including The Cellar, Durban's oldest and busiest 'supper theatre' venue.

Johannesburg:

Agfa Theatre on the Square

Sandton Square, Sandton. Tel: (011) 883 8606. Intimate venue staging all kinds of productions, from drama to musicals.

The Market Theatre Complex

Newtown Cultural Precinct, Bree and Wolhuter Sts, Newtown. Tel: (011) 836 1648. The home of anti-apartheid theatre in the 1970s and 80s, now a thriving arts complex which includes three theatres.

Pretoria:

State Theatre

320 Pretorius St, City Centre. Tel: (012) 322 1665. One of South Africa's leading performance venues.

Arts festivals

The Western Cape:

Klein Karoo Nasionale Kunstefees

Oudtshoorn. Tel: (044) 272 7771. Last week in Mar (ring for details). All facets of the arts from theatre and music to fine arts and crafts, with special attention paid to Afrikaner talent.

Spier Festival

Spier Wine Estate, Lynedoch Rd, Stellenbosch (R310). Tel: (021) 434 5423. Nov–Mar (ring for exact dates).

Offers opera, jazz, chamber music, dance and stand-up comedy. Main venue is the sizeable Spier Amphitheatre.

Stellenbosch Festival of Music and the Arts

Tel: (021) 883 3891. Late Sept (ring for exact dates). The programme for this prestigious annual festival includes symphony concerts, master classes, ensemble recitals, art exhibitions and craft markets. Main venues are Endler Hall and the Conservatoire, Stellenbosch University.

The Eastern Cape:

The Standard Bank National Arts Festival

Grahamstown. Tel: (046) 622 7115. Website: www.sbfest.co.za. First fortnight in July (ring for exact dates). South Africa's biggest and best annual cultural jamboree, an event which sees every venue in this old Settler city – from the giant 1820 Settler's Monument on the outskirts of town to the scout hall – buzzing with activity. While the main programme features student theatre, a book fair and jazz and film festivals alongside formal performances of drama, music and dance, the Fringe attracts experimental talent. And don't miss the buskers and craft markets, either.

KwaZulu-Natal:

Artfest

Durban. Tel: (031) 304 4934. July (ring for details). Annual showcase for the visual and performing arts and culture.

Durban International Film Festival

Elizabeth Sneddon Theatre, Unviersity of Natal, Durban. Tel: (031) 260 2594. Last week in July. South Africa's largest, longest-running non-profit film festival, showcasing international features and shorts as well as homegrown works.

Gauteng:

Arts Alive

Various venues, Greater Johannesburg. Tel: (011) 838 6405. Sept–Oct. Jo'burg welcomes the spring with this month-long celebration of the performing arts.

FNB Vita Dance Umbrella

Wits University Theatre, Jorissen St, Braamfontein. Tel: (011) 442 8435. Feb–Mar. Contemporary dance festival which aims to foster new talent. Performers include community groups as well as professional dance companies.

Booking tickets

With more than 300 branches countrywide, **Computicket** sells tickets for most entertainment and leisure events in South Africa, from movies to classical music concerts and sporting events.
Johannesburg: *tel: (011) 331 9991.*
Cape Town: *tel: (021) 21 4715.*
Durban: *tel: (031) 304 4881.*
Pretoria: *tel: (012) 322 7650.*
Ticketline (*tel: (011) 445 8200; open daily 0900–2000*) takes advance bookings for credit card holders only.

179

Practical information

PRACTICAL INFORMATION

Practical information

Airports

South Africa's main airport, **Johannesburg International**, is 30km east of Jo'burg and 60km from Pretoria. Other international airports are at **Cape Town** (about 20km from the city) and **Durban** (16km). All three are served by regular bus services to the city centres, while many of the larger hotels also provide courtesy buses for their guests. Taxis are plentiful and comparatively inexpensive, although do check the meter is running at the start of the journey. All the major car-hire companies are represented at these airports.

Climate

South Africa's seasons are the reverse of those in the UK, with midwinter in June and July and midsummer in December and January.

The Highveld – especially the Gauteng area – has a fabulous climate with year-round sunshine. Hot summers are cooled by dramatic late-afternoon thunderstorms, while winters are bright and dry. It can get surprisingly chilly at night, though.

Cape Town and the southern part of the **Western Cape** has Mediterranean-style weather, with mild, changeable winters (when most of the rainfall occurs), and warm to roasting summers. Locals say the nicest time is March to May, when the wind drops, the sun shines – and most tourists have gone home!

Durban and the **KwaZulu-Natal** coasts enjoy a steamy subtropical climate, again with plenty of sunshine year round. Down at sea level, summers are hot, thundery and humid. Best months to visit are June and July, when the humidity is at its lowest.

Currency

South Africa's currency unit is the **Rand**, denoted by the symbol **R**. It's divided into 100 **cents (c)**. Bank notes are issued in denominations of R200, R100, R50, R20 and R10, while coins come in 1, 2, 10, 20, and 50c; R1 and R2. At the time of going to press, the exchange rate was approximately £1 = R10 and US$1 = R7.

Customs regulations

You're allowed to bring R5000 cash into the country. Unlimited foreign currency and travellers' cheques are allowed, however, provided you declare it on arrival. Foreign passport-holders may not take out more foreign currency than they declared on arrival.

Duty-free allowances: 400 cigarettes, 250g tobacco and 50 cigars, one litre of spirit, two litres of wine, 50ml perfume and 250ml toilet water.

You also won't pay duty on gifts, souvenirs and other goods up to the value of R500.

Disabled travellers

South Africa's disabled facilities are still quite limited, although the situation is improving. The **South African Tourism Board (Satour)** publishes an accommodation guide including information on hotels with facilities for disabled people (*see page 15 for Satour's details*). The **Sports Science Institute of South Africa** can provide details of activities and tours, such as the braille and wheelchair trails now established in various national parks and nature reserves. *Tel: 0027 212 686 7330 (ext 297).*

Electricity

Urban power systems are generally 220/230 volts AC (250V in Pretoria). Most hotel rooms are equipped with sockets which will take a 110V electric razor, but you'll need a three-point round-pin transformer plug if you want to use any other electrical appliances here.

Entry formalities

Visitors from the **UK**, the **US**, **Canada**, **Australia** and **New Zealand** (as well as other countries such as Ireland, Germany and Japan) do not need a visa to visit South Africa, just a valid passport and a valid return ticket. You'll be issued with an entry permit on arrival, and you may also be asked to prove that you have sufficient funds to cover your stay. EU nationals with a valid passport may stay in South Africa for up to six months.

If you do need a visa, you must apply at the South African embassy or consulate in your own country several weeks before you plan to depart. If you're including **Lesotho** or **Swaziland** in your itinerary, ask for a multiple-entry visa.

South African Embassies and Missions Abroad:

Australia: *Rhodes Place, Yarralumla, Canberra ACT 2600. Tel: (02) 6273 2424.*
Canada: *15 Sussex Drive, Ottawa K1M 1M8. Tel: (613) 744 0330.*
UK: *South Africa House, Trafalgar Square, London WC2N 5DP. Tel: (0171) 930 4488.*
US: *3051 Massachusetts Ave NW, Washington DC 20008. Tel: (202) 232 4400. Suite 300, 50 North La Cienega Blvd, Beverly Hills, CA 90211. Tel: (213) 657 9200.*

Health

Travellers face few serious health risks in South Africa. Standards of hygiene are generally high, and it's safe to drink the water in all tourist areas.

Sunburn is probably the most common health hazard, simply because many visitors don't realise just how dangerous the sun can be. If you're exposed to too much ultraviolet radiation (UVR), you run the risk of contracting skin cancer in later life, so start off with short

Northern Province. The Northern Cape's **Kalahari Gemsbok Park** is a low-risk area. If you're planning to visit, consult your doctor for advice on the most suitable prophylactic before you travel. Once you're there, sleep under a **mosquito net** if possible, and during the day cover all exposed parts with **mosquito repellent**, preferably one containing diethyltoluamide. Burning **mosquito coils** is a good idea, too.

Snakes and insects – snakes are not often sighted (they're fast movers) and most bites are not fatal. If you are bitten, however, the worst thing to do is panic: try to memorise what the snake looked like, wrap the bitten limb as tightly as possible and get to the nearest clinic or hospital.

Ticks are a more common hazard, particularly if you're walking in the bush through long grass. Minute pepper ticks are the worst, leaving nasty welts that can itch for months. If you plan to go hiking, use a good insect repellent or spray before you set off. If you are bitten, a dab of alcohol or Vaseline will persuade a tick to let go. As for **spiders**, most are harmless and should simply be left alone.

Vaccinations: none are compulsory, although you should take the precaution of ensuring you are up to date with your boosters for tetanus and polio.

Information

Most towns in South Africa have a tourist information office where you can pick up travel advice, maps and lists of accommodation. See the destinations section of the guide for details of local offices, (*and pages 15–16 for the regional tourist authorities*).

daily doses of sun which you gradually increase. Use a **high protection sunscreen** (Factor 15, or at least 25 if your skin is fair) and wear a sunhat and sunglasses designed to absorb at least 95 per cent UVR. While you're acclimatising to the higher temperatures you should also drink plenty of water (at least a litre a day) in order to avoid dehydration.

AIDS is widespread in South Africa in both men and women. Your chances of catching the virus through unprotected sex are good – so use a condom.

Malaria is spread through mosquito bites. While not infectious, it's potentially dangerous (even fatal) without treatment. Symptoms include high fever, chills, headaches and sweating, all in waves.

Most of South Africa's **malarial areas** are in the northeast of the country, specifically **Mpumalanga** (including the Kruger National Park), **northern KwaZulu-Natal** (including Hluhluwe-Umfolozi Game Reserve) and parts of

185

South Africa on the web:

www.freedom.co.za The history of Robben Island, the notorious Alcatraz-like island where Nelson Mandela was held prisoner for 27 years.

www.mg.co.za/mg The weekly *Mail & Guardian* newspaper's website makes a good introduction to the country, with lots of links to other sites and some useful travel information.

www.saa.co.za The official South African Airways website, with current departure and arrival times, prices and routes.

www.southafrica.co.za South Africa Online claims to be the Internet gateway into the country. It's a reasonable claim – links to other sites abound, covering everything from the weather to newspapers and nightclubs.

www.touristoffices.org.uk/South_Africa The South African Tourist Board's official website offers information on airlines, tour operators, car hire and visas.

Insurance

It's a good idea to take out a travel insurance policy covering at least **lost or stolen baggage** and **medical costs** before you visit South Africa. Most tour operators and travel agents will arrange insurance for you when you book, although it pays to shop around. If you want to take part in adventure activities such as abseiling, watersports or hiking, check the policy to make sure you're covered – you may have to pay an extra premium.

Maps

Good maps are widely available from regional and local tourist offices as well as the better bookshops.

Opening times

Banks: Mon–Fri 0900–1530, Sat 0830–1100.

Bars: Mon–Sat 0900–1100, closing later in the major cities. On Sundays, you usually have to buy a meal if you want a drink.

Museums: Mon–Fri 1000–1700, open daily in the larger cities.

Petrol stations: daily 0700–1900, although some open round the clock.

Restaurants: generally, Tue–Sun 1200–1500, 1900–2130 (kitchen closing time).

Shops and businesses: Mon–Fri 0800–1630, Sat 0830–1230.

Tourist offices: generally, Mon–Fri 0830–1300, 1400–1700, Sat 0900–1200.

Public holidays

1 Jan	New Year's Day
21 Mar	Human Rights Day
Mar/Apr	Good Friday, Easter Sunday and Easter Monday
27 Apr	Freedom Day
1 May	Workers' Day
16 June	Youth Day
9 Aug	National Woman's Day
24 Sept	Heritage Day
16 Dec	Day of Reconciliation
25 Dec	Christmas Day
26 Dec	Day of Goodwill

Reading

Fiction

July's People, Nadine Gordimer (Penguin). The Nobel Prizewinner turns her ruthlessly honest eye on the complex power-relations between master and servant – in this case, a liberal white family and their black gardener, July.

The Smell of Apples, Mark Behr (Abacus). This story of a white boy growing up in Cape Town during the ultra-militaristic 1960s and 70s is told in a deceptively simple style.

Autobiography

My Traitor's Heart, Rian Malan (Vintage). Compelling personal account by an Afrikaner trying to come to terms with his heritage.

Long Walk to Freedom, Nelson Mandela (Abacus). Best-selling account of the former president's life, and especially poignant on his years in prison.

History

The Boer War, Thomas Pakenham (Abacus). The definitive account. Grippingly written, with the narrative pace of a novel.

The Mind of South Africa, Allister Sparks (Penguin). Thought-provoking overview of South Africa's turbulent history by one of the country's most respected journalists.

Safety and security

Although violent crime is a serious problem in South Africa's major centres – especially Johannesburg – most visitors come and go without incident. Paranoia is not necessary, common sense is.

- In **cities**, don't go out on the streets carrying a camera or wearing expensive jewellery, watches or sunglasses.
- Don't carry more **money** than you actually need (but always have some to hand over in case you are mugged).
- Don't get drawn into conversation at **ATM** machines, no matter how well-spoken the other person is, and never allow anyone to see your PIN number.

directory enquiry service (*tel: 1023*). South Africa's international access code is **27** (preceded by 00 from the UK, 011 from the US and Canada, and 0011 from Australia). To dial out once you're there, the international access code is **09**.

Time

South African Standard Time is two hours ahead of GMT, seven hours ahead of US Eastern Standard Time, and eight hours behind Australian Eastern Standard Time.

Tipping

A 12–15 per cent tip is customary in restaurants if the service has been good. In hotels, R10 is reasonable for the concierge, the valet parking attendant and the cleaning staff. You should tip the concierge more for service beyond the call of duty, such as locating tickets for a sold-out show.

- **Drive** with the doors locked and the windows rolled up, and don't leave your bag in view on the seat.

Telephones

Public call boxes are widely available in cities and towns, and increasingly in the rural areas, too. **Phonecards** in various denominations can be purchased from post offices and newsagents. **Mobile phones** (known as cellphones here) can be hired from the airports in the major centres and in the cities themselves. Hotels add a (usually huge) surcharge to your calls. If you have problems getting through, try the free

Toilets

In the cities, malls, large hotels or (if you ask nicely) restaurants are probably your best bet. Keep a few R2 coins handy to tip the attendant. On the road, look out for the larger petrol stations-cum-rest-stops.

189

Index

191

Editorial, design and production credits

Project management: Dial House Publishing Services
Series editor: Christopher Catling
Copy editor: Posy Gosling
Proof-reader: Posy Gosling
Picture research: Image Select International

Series and cover design: Trickett & Webb Limited
Cover artwork: Wenham Arts
Text layout: Wenham Arts
Map work: RJS Associates

Repro and image setting: Z2 Repro, Thetford, Norfolk, UK
Printed and bound by: Artes Graficas ELKAR S. Coop., Bilbao, Spain

We would like to thank the following photographers and organisations for the photographs used in this book, to whom the copyright in the photographs belong:

Image Select (pages 4, 97 and 134); Spectrum (pages 6, 9, 16, 29, 44, 63B, 79, 101, 107, 109, 120A, 126, 146, 166, 168 and 187A); South African Tourism Board (page 7, 11, 24, 54, 55, 62, 64, 72, 78, 91B, 99, 110, 118, 120B, 128, 139, 153, 157, 173, 185 and 186); Loretta Steyn (page 8); Hein von Horsten (pages 10, 26, 46, 144, 172 and 184); Ellen Elmendorp (page 12); Paul Velasco (page 13); Telegraph Colour Library (pages 14, 163, 174, 179 and 180); Shaen Adey (pages 15, 37, 38, 85, 90, 117, 160 and 177); Anthony Bannister (pages 19, 63A, 142 and 155); Gallo Images (page 20); Roger de la Harpe (pages 27, 74, 84, 91A, 96, 132, 133, 167, 169, 188A, 188B and 189); Martin Harvey (pages 31, 48 and 182); Lanz von Horsten (pages 3 and 67); E Thiel (page 42); Rod Haestier (page 43); Gus van Dyk (page 56); Peter Lillie (pages 60, 81 and 151); Lorna Stanton (pages 71, 150 and 162); Peter Pinnock (page 83); Phillip Richardson (page 92); Emma Borg (page 103); Brenda Ryan (page 108); Lisa Trocchi (pages 115 and 171); Struik Image Library (page 116); Andrew Bannister (pages 127 and 176); Luke Hunter (page 135); Keith Beg (page 136); Nigel J Dennis (page 145); Paul Funston (page 138); Gerald Hinde (page 152); Carol Hughes (page 154); Planet Earth Pictures (page 156); John Bracegirdle (page 164); Colorific (page 170); J Allan Cash (page 175); Ken Oosterbroek (page 178); Robert C Nunnington (page 187B).

Acknowledgements: The author would like to thank the following for their invaluable assistance: South African Airways and Thomas Cook Holidays.